So You Think You're Ready For College?

Critical College Skills That Don't Show Up On A College Application

Kent T. Cubbage, Ph.D.

DEDICATION

This book is dedicated to my parents and former teachers at Alton Senior High School in Alton, Illinois, who gave me most of the wisdom in this book. Thanks also for giving me the skills to write a book like this someday.

CONTENTS

ACKNOWLEDGMENTS

Special thanks to Cheryl Black, Edison College (Florida) and Dr. Paul Leslie, Aiken Technical College (South Carolina) for their help, inspiration and insight.

Thanks as well to Stephanie Lockwood for the cover art.

Preface I: For You College-Bound High School Students (And Those Already In College)

Congratulations! You have matriculated. I hope that word was on the SAT. Hard work and determination are required to succeed in college. I know you exhibited these attributes to get into college, and maybe you sacrificed countless additional hours to get accepted into an elite university. There may have been A.P. courses, extracurricular activities, standardized test training, a great GPA, and putting on your best Shakespeare with college application essays. Then again, you may have chosen the community or career college route, as it best suits your goals. Either way, you're now a college student.

Soon you'll be sitting in a classroom with professors like me in front of you. For starters, please don't forget that at one time we professors were all at the point where you are now. I've had struggling students say to me, "This is easy for you. You're the *professor*."

Believe me, there were no warp drives that transported us from high school to our Ph.D. dissertation defenses. Don't think it all came easy. Don't think for a minute we aced every class we took. If I could take my calculus grade off my undergraduate transcript I'd do it today. You may have professors who literally wrote the book – the same, expensive book you have to buy for a class – even though he or she barely earned a "C" in that subject back in the day. (That professor, moreover, is getting very little of the $200 you paid for it.) Every tenured, full professor was a college freshman once, no different from you in most ways.

But we professors will be the first to say that many things have changed dramatically since we were students, setting you apart from our earlier generations. I earned my bachelor's and master's degrees in the 1990s. It wasn't *that* long ago. The Simpsons were on TV while I was in college, just like you, but there was no internet during my four years as a undergrad. E-mail came about just as I finished my master's. Between finishing my master's in 1993 and completing my Ph.D. in 2009, smartphones, tablets, Google, Wi-Fi, GIS, and so many other things you may take for granted became commonplace. This explosion in technology has made the college experience much more complicated.

Someone who graduated college just twenty years ago would likely not recognize his or her alma mater's campus now. Colleges and universities have been on construction sprees, putting up new buildings as fast as they can build them. Many of these glossy new buildings house departments and services that are all recent concoctions, including "development" (fundraising), counseling, and diversity/inclusion. Some of these buildings are nicer than classroom buildings, and they are filled with armies of staff and administrators that have little to do with the classroom. At some point you'll hear the older professors complain about this. Just smile and nod.

The bottom line is that without the proper skills, and some "inside" knowledge, it will be overwhelming to know how to survive and thrive on the modern college campus. It will be difficult to figure out how to communicate appropriately with a professor, especially because you have so many ways to communicate these days. It can be scary knowing you may come out of college with heavy debt, also a relatively new phenomenon. This debt, moreover, will only grow larger if you make mistakes with course selection, you do not keep up with advising, or you keep changing majors.

For centuries there were only traditional lecture courses. Course formats these days include online, MOOC, hybrid, and flipped courses. It's a dizzying array of options that can be extremely confusing.

I've been in the trenches at four colleges and universities. I've seen first-hand the things you need to know as a college student that won't show up on your college applications. That is what this book is designed to help with. It will become apparent that what you learned in AP physics or SAT prep wasn't enough to succeed in college. You will likely have a short orientation the summer before you begin school, and you may be required to take a college-orientation course during your first semester. But it's much better to have the skills to run the race before the race begins.

Colleagues told me that I needed to include flashy graphics and cute pictures in this book to keep young readers' attention. Most things in life will not be flashy and cute, so you won't find those graphics or pictures in this book. Hopefully I'll give you a laugh or two along the way, but you'll note that many times my advice will hit you right between the eyes, with no frills. That's because I don't want you to make mistakes when it really matters. Those who have told you that it's best to learn from your mistakes were wrong. It's best to learn from *other people's mistakes*. I'll teach you the skills to do this. These skills are absolutely essential, but you can certainly master them. Soon you'll be in class with professors like me, and we'll know if you did!

Preface II: For You Students Returning To College After Time Away

Congratulations, and welcome back to college! I know that you are anxious about returning to school. I've taught hundreds of students who returned to college after time away. I've never met one who wasn't apprehensive about it. Maybe you have "empty nested" and want a new career. Maybe you are back because you have had a traumatic life event, such as a divorce. It's possible that the factory where you have worked for years has recently been shuttered. There are those of you who went to college right after high school at your parents' insistence, only to party, slack, and flunk out. Now, several years later, you realize what a foolish kid you were and regret the opportunity you squandered. You want a second chance.

You will be among teenage students in your classes and, at age thirty, forty, or even older, it will feel strange sitting next to them. They may be the same age as your younger siblings, or your children. You may have grandchildren their ages. You may hear the occasional snicker from the younger students about how seriously you take every aspect of your studies, and you'll wonder how so many of them can take it all so lightly, especially given the money being spent on their education.

You'll feel inferior on the first day of class because the newbie students surrounding you just received an "up-to-date" high school education. After all, they just took calculus and AP biology, right? They have never known life without a computer. You couldn't program the VCR for all of those years.

I've seen the entire gamut, and I know your fears. But they are unfounded. Ask any professor, and he or she will tell you that "non-traditional" students are always among the best. You have traits that only experience can bestow: wisdom, poise, seeing the big picture. You have perspective on life and, as such, you will have perspective on school. Best of all, you know the value of that most elusive of things... *time*.

You may eventually realize that your high school education from the 1960s or 1970s, one that contained no AP courses, no technology, and no college-entrance exams, was superior in many ways to the high school education the younger students just received. After the first exam, which you'll likely ace, you'll have some of the younger students want to study with you. They will complain less when they see a working mother of three earn the best grades in the class.

Despite this pep talk, many things have changed since you were in college, even if it was only a few years back. Among these are technology (such as e-books), modes of communication, and the myriad of campus services. There is now a new palette of course-delivery methods, including online, MOOC, hybrid, and flipped courses. Even traditional lecture courses may have an internet component.

I'm sure you very much value your money at this point in your life and don't want to waste a penny. Not knowing how to best invest those dollars on a modern college campus can and will be costly. Many newer classes place a bigger emphasis on teamwork and group discussion than when you were last in school, and knowing how to make the most of those situations is a must.

It's critical that you are properly prepared for these scenarios. That's where I come in. This book will provide you with a roadmap, and the tools you'll need, for your successful return to college. The younger students will have much to learn from you, and both younger and older students will learn much from these pages. This book is laced with levity, but you'll find that the information I'm trying to impart is no-nonsense. Many of you are parents, so I know you'll appreciate the occasional tough talk!

Preface III: For The Parents

Congratulations! You are the parents of a college student. Maybe you have many more in the pipeline. Remember all those vacations you skimped on, or skipped altogether? How about that 2000 Taurus you keep driving even though the air conditioning has failed? That money you saved will be paying for the likes of Psych 101, room and board, and textbooks. In fact, most of it will go towards textbooks. When you get the bill for your child's textbooks you might be inclined to think that the campus bookstore sells only first editions of Gutenberg's Bible. Times have changed.

And, wow, how they have changed. My father grew up during the Depression in a relatively poor and unstable household in the metropolis of Oxford Junction, Iowa, population 300 (give or take a dozen). In those days, college was considered a luxury for the "fancy people," as he called them. It was a privilege reserved for, well, the privileged. College was never a part of family conversation in my father's household. This was the case throughout most of the country, but especially the case for hayseeds from farm country like my old man. In his world, you were fully absorbed into the family farm or you joined the military after high school.

My father left the house the day after his high school graduation, one of a whopping nine graduates at his high school that year, and worked on the railroads for a few years. The hot sun and a sore back gave him plenty to think about. One day he heard about something that would change the trajectory of the country as much as the war did: the Servicemen's Readjustment Act, better known as the G.I. Bill, which President Franklin Roosevelt signed into law in 1944. It was born out of necessity as a way to deal with the millions of servicemen returning from the war, but it was revolutionary.

It occurred to my father that he could serve his country for four years and have his college education paid for. He promptly joined the Air Force, served four years, and graduated from the University of Iowa in three and a half years. He was the first and only one in my family to graduate from college until I did in the early 1990s.

The differences between my family and my wife's family could not be more striking. Think the Clampetts versus the Kennedys. Nowhere is this more evident than in classroom exploits. When my father was a wide-eyed college student at the University of Iowa in the 1950s, my wife's grandmother was already a college graduate in neighboring Minnesota. It's easy to forget how unusual that was generations ago. Your kids would probably be surprised to find out that the average great-grandmother was several times more likely to be a homemaker than a college graduate. Today, women make up more than 50% of all medical and law students!

The rest of my wife's family continued the trend. Her father has a law degree and her mother has a master's degree. Her aunt and uncle have Ph.Ds. from Boston University and MIT, respectively. One of their children is a Harvard-trained neurologist and the other graduated from Carnegie Mellon. The rest of my wife's family tree has professionals from all walks of life, with all manner of diplomas on the wall. Get-togethers with her family were something I had to adjust to early in our marriage. Their affluence reflects their scholarly achievement. They drink expensive wine, do the New York Times crossword puzzle before most people wake up, and talk about things like Renaissance art and Egyptology. At my family get-togethers you can learn how to get on disability or plea to a lesser charge.

Parents, you may find yourself from a family like mine, a family like my wife's, or somewhere in between, but the bottom line is that your child is headed to college. Whether your child is the first in your family to go to college or you have a long Ivy League pedigree, one thing is certain: it's a big deal. With the cost of college skyrocketing and fewer jobs for college graduates than in previous generations, there is less room for error in this endeavor.

These days a college education is so often an expectation – an expectation of the family, of the high school, and of our society at large. Although I'm an academic, I'm conflicted about the mantra of "college for all." If you've ever waited a week for a plumber to fix your leaking faucet or sat next to a space heater for days before an HVAC tech could get to your house, you may be inclined to agree. But that's the subject of another book. This book is about the student getting a college education as the expectation, but more importantly, *it's about the expectations of the student while getting a college education.*

While attributes such as resourcefulness and hard work will always play in a college student's favor, the college experience is substantially different than it was even in the 1990s, radically different in many regards. Technology and social media have consumed and transformed young lives – sometimes for the better, but sometimes not. I have witnessed this revolution from the front row. Technology has put the world at young people's feet, but it has blurred the lines between appropriate and inappropriate communication. Students say things to me on a weekly basis that would have been unthinkable to say to a professor when I was an undergraduate. This behavior isn't just from first-in-the-family college students who don't have a role model or mentor from whom to learn college classroom decorum. I see it also from students who went to elite high schools and graduated with honors.

There are many examples in the pages that follow.

Modes of course-content delivery have changed. New areas of study have mushroomed. Colleges and universities offer a smorgasbord of services that did not exist a generation ago. You'll be paying for them.

You've done a great job, parents, as evidenced by your child getting accepted to college and standing on the cusp of potentially great things. I know you have done everything to prepare them not only for college, but also for life. Yet, if hybrid, online, and flipped courses are new to you, you may have no frame of reference to prepare your kids to succeed in them. If dorm spas, disability coordinators, diversity and inclusion officers, and the like weren't around in your day, it's a challenge to know how to best utilize them.

Your child likely had or will have a short college orientation during the summer before freshman year. Many colleges also offer a college-orientation course during the first semester. I had one as a freshman, back in 1987. It was taught by a senior who essentially said, "Study hard and don't party too much." The average orientation course has become more in-depth these days and is certainly more useful than the one I took. Nonetheless, it's a much more desirable situation for your college-bound student to have the skills to navigate the modern institution of higher learning *before he or she enters it*. These are essential, not optional, tools to limit the on-the-job training and learning curve of the new college student. This book may be the one used in the orientation course your child is required to take during freshman year. If so, he or she is ahead of the game.

Bookstores and online retailers have libraries full of books on how to study for the SAT, how to fill out a college application, how to write an essay, and so forth. This is not one of those books. I present skills and knowledge that won't show up on a college application, but are every bit as critical.

While this book is written with the student as the audience (frequently referencing "you," the student), I strongly urge you parents to read it for yourselves. Do this preferably before your child reads the book, and you can discuss the advice and information herein either chapter by chapter or when your child finishes the read. If you already have kids in college, read the book and send it to them.

Much of my advice comes sprinkled with humor. Many times it is pointed and direct, even occasionally a tad harsh. In those instances that is my exact intention. Much is at stake with college attendance these days, and my help is commensurate with the stakes at hand. The cute, flashy pictures that some of my colleagues had suggested I include for the younger students would only serve to distract them from the importance of the information and advice I provide.

Bear in mind also that higher education is a sprawling enterprise, with literally thousands of colleges and universities in existence. There are large public universities, small liberal arts colleges, faith-based institutions, for-profit colleges, colleges that cater to women and minorities, and community/junior colleges, to name a few. Each institution will do things a bit differently. Although I will give you the basics in this book, you and your child will need to research and work within the rules, policies and traditions of the particular school your child attends.

Life comes with precious few guarantees. Books certainly do not. However, if your child reads this book and implements the advice and tips I present, his or her college experience will go more smoothly. There will be fewer headaches, less wasted time, and a much better overall experience. Don't be surprised if you save some money along the way as well. Then maybe you can finally get rid of the 2000 Taurus – and trade it in for a 2005 until the kids are out of college.

Chapter 1: University GPS: Getting Intimately Familiar With The Campus

It's logical that you'd think the first day of the semester corresponds to the first day of classes on your schedule, but you'd be wrong. If you think that's the case, you'll probably be late for the first day of classes. I've taught approximately 175 sections of various courses over the last fifteen years. On 175 occasions some students were late for the first day of class. Even if you think you've successfully slinked into the back of a large classroom without being noticed, your professor saw you. We have a sixth sense when it comes to our classroom. Don't forget that we manage classrooms for a living. If you are one of the tardy students, you have drawn negative attention to yourself before you've taken your first note. That is not the way you want to start the semester.

I see dozens of students during the first week of the semester who are clearly lost. You can spot them easily. Just look down the hallway for the students who keep squinting at a piece of paper in their hands while continually looking up at door numbers. At some point they panic and frantically ask for directions. They are usually on the wrong floor and sometimes in the wrong building. A closer look at their schedule reveals that they are *late for class*. I take pity on these students and ask if they need help. I tease them a little to ease their stress, remarking that, "If you were lost any longer, there would be an Amber Alert." Despite the outward kindness on my part in those situations, I'm not impressed by the lapse in responsibility.

1.1 Understanding Your Class Schedule

You can easily avoid getting lost while looking for your classrooms. *Read your class schedule carefully.* Be sure that you know the correct days and times for each class. Don't make any assumptions during the first week of classes.

I teach a course with a lecture and lab that meet on separate days. Without fail, a student shows up in the lecture room on the day we have lab, and vice versa, and gets upset because he or she thinks class was cancelled. Occasionally these students assume that I didn't show up and go tell the Department Chair or Dean. If you ever want to get into a professor's doghouse, make this mistake! It's also common for some students to disturb everybody in a class that has started by abruptly leaving when they realize they have misread their schedules and are in the wrong room.

If you signed up for a class with a lab component, don't assume that you won't meet for lab the first week. I have no idea how that notion keeps persisting, but many students won't show for the first lab.

1.2 Knowing Your Way Around Campus

A few days before class, *use a campus map to visit every building and every classroom on your schedule*. The map should be easy to pull up on a portable device. You don't want to be walking aimlessly around a cavernous building on the first day of class when you thought you'd find the classroom easily. Many older buildings have odd or downright wacky room numbering that takes forever to figure out. There were times when I thought I needed a degree in cryptology to determine where to go in certain campus buildings. Sometimes a class gets moved to another room or building at the last minute. This happens frequently if there is a scheduling conflict with another class that went unnoticed, the college is remodeling classrooms, or classes in better facilities have been cancelled and the professor wants a nicer room. If you go a day early you may see a note on the door to that effect, and can plan on being at the new classroom on time.

I often ask tardy students why they were late for the first day of class. Some of the typical answers involve transportation problems that could have been avoided. The most common reply is, "I couldn't find a parking space." To which I answer, "Did you not factor in the other five hundred students trying to squeeze into fifty spaces today?" Other answers include, "The buses were full..." or "I thought the bus came to this building..." or "I thought it was only a five-minute walk from my dorm."

Some of you might attend colleges with large campuses. I graduated from a Big Ten university whose campus sprawls out over two cities. I was stunned by the countless heads bobbing up and down when I walked the campus quad for the first time. It looked as though a football game had just let out. It was not uncommon to walk thirty minutes to class, depending on where you lived, and there were many times that I had to jog to my next class because it was a fifteen-minute walk and I only had ten minutes. A scooter made short work of this during my senior year. In cold climates you can often walk to your classes for part of the semester (or ride a scooter), but you'll need to take the bus or other transit in the colder months. If this is the case, ride that bus route before the first day you need to so that you are familiar with the route.

Find your classrooms before the first day of class, *but also practice getting there using the same mode of transportation you'll use throughout the semester*. Factor in the madness of first-week traffic, both car and foot. If you get there really early, you may be able to introduce yourself to the professor or teaching assistant and give a good first impression before the class even starts. Think of the poor impression you'll give if you're late on the first day. The professor will think, "How can this student have what it takes to pass this challenging class if he or she can't read a simple schedule?" You don't want to show up late for work, and they are paying *you*. Why would you show up late for class when you are the one paying?

Follow these guidelines every semester, even if you think you know campus inside and out. You'll likely move from dorm to apartment or sorority house to rental house, and your routes to class are going to change. Don't be the one standing in the hall – confused and in need of an Amber Alert – on the first day of classes.

Chapter 2: The Academic Trifecta: Choosing A Major, Getting Advised, And Registering For Classes

There are endless choices when it comes to where you can attend college. You may have a hard time deciding what type of institution you want to attend, and eventually boil your choices down to small liberal arts colleges or large research universities. Then again, you may know exactly what type of college you want to attend, such as a faith-based college, and narrow your choices down to, for example, a few Catholic institutions. Regardless of where you attend, you'll be required to declare a major at some point. You will be assigned an academic advisor to help guide you in that major. And there is no escaping the duty of formally signing up for classes each semester. Let's take a look at the elements in that chain of events.

2.1 Choosing A Major

"What's your major?" That's a question you'll get asked by friends, family, bosses and classmates hundreds of times over the course of your college years. Ironically, for most of the history of higher education in the United States and abroad, all college graduates earned the exact same degree. College study traditionally consisted of reading and analyzing the great works of Western literature, often in classical Greek and Latin. There were no elective courses, no voluminous course catalogs, and no majors. This changed dramatically over the last century. These days a college student can choose from thousands of courses and hundreds of majors.

I had the good fortune of knowing exactly what I wanted to major in before I started college. I was enthralled with the natural world as a child. My backyard was a huge Boy Scout camp that served as my personal laboratory. I'd set out into the camp woods to identify the woodland wildflowers. I marveled at the insides of the fish I caught in the camp lake when I cleaned them with my fillet knife. I photographed and measured the beaver huts in the camp streams. There was no doubt about what I was going to study in college, and I tailored my high school classes towards my desired college major. You guessed it – biology.

Some of you are equally as lucky. You may have known what you wanted to study in college since you were a young boy or girl. I suspect that most college-bound students are at least partially unsure about what subject they'll major in, and many have no clue whatsoever. Choosing a major can be a complicated process. It's not made any easier by those who tell you what you should major in.

Back in the mid-1980s everybody said, "Major in business. You can't go wrong. The field is going to explode." A few years later there was a glut of business majors. Not long after that, everybody said to major in computers. Soon thereafter, IT professionals were getting laid off left and right. In recent years, everybody has recommended majoring in health care. In a decade or so, a glut of health-care workers – combined with newer technology – may lead to difficulty finding a job in those fields. Who knows if that will happen, but following the herd is always a bad idea.

When I was an undergrad I was told that most students shouldn't major in anything specific. "Employers want you to be able to do different things," I heard. "They just want to know that you can learn, so be a generalist." By the time I graduated, we were all being told that we needed to major in something specific. "The world is getting more specialized. Employers want you to know a particular subject," was the refrain. This conventional wisdom isn't always wise, and the workplace is always changing. Stay as far away from it as you can.

Choosing a major is a very personal decision. It should be done based on what is important to you. If you choose a major based on what others insist upon, you'll be miserable. First, you'll loathe college. Do you want to spend the next several years studying something that doesn't interest you? You'll just end up changing your major and starting over, having wasted credit hours and tuition dollars. If you graduate with a degree in something you don't really enjoy, chances are that those who did enjoy it earned better grades and will be more successful at finding jobs.

While I stand by this advice, there are caveats. I always say, "Follow your heart, but use your head." Try to study something you are passionate about, but be realistic about how far it can take you in the future. Philosophy is a cool major, but you'll probably wait tables the rest of your life. Theater might sound intriguing, but how many people actually earn a living acting?

You may have heard the saying, "Do something you love and you'll never work a day in your life." I am a firm believer in that advice, but the cold truth is that most people aren't head over heels in love with their jobs. Your career path starts with your major. If you find a subject that does interest you – one that makes you look forward to signing up for the next semester of classes – you're on the right track.

I stress the importance of studying something you enjoy, but don't panic if you are college bound and don't have the foggiest idea what you want to major in. At most colleges you don't have to declare a major during your freshman year. Take a wide variety of courses to see what piques your interest. Ask your roommates and friends about their majors and why they chose them. You should be concerned only if you don't want to study anything in particular after your freshman year. I knew scores of fellow students who couldn't decide on a major because they floated through their first several semesters blithely taking courses, and never really explored classes that actually interested them.

In contrast, there are those of you who are passionate about two or more subjects. Once you've chosen a major, you might be tempted to declare a minor as well. Definitely go for it if you fall into this category. There are many benefits to a major/minor course of study. Potential employers will know that you chose a more difficult path, and that you love to learn. It gives you flexibility in your job search. It will arm you with additional practical knowledge if you want to continue your education beyond your bachelor's degree. I've known many people who majored in biology and minored in chemistry, with designs on medical or veterinary school. It paid huge dividends on their entrance exams and applications. A minor in a language is a great idea if you eventually want to work abroad.

If you do decide to minor in something, be prepared to put in the extra work. You'll definitely be looking at sixteen or more credit hours every semester. Summer classes may be unavoidable. There will be more late nights studying. But in the end you won't regret it. I was within shouting distance of a minor in German. I could have earned it with a few more conversational German classes that would have easily squeezed into summers and my senior year. I talked myself out of it and have regretted it ever since.

2.2 The Academic Advisement Process

The advising concept varies among colleges and universities. Some colleges have an advisement center full of dedicated, non-faculty advisors where all students come to be advised. Larger universities often have non-faculty advisors who advise students in a particular major or program. Smaller colleges and many community colleges will assign you to a faculty advisor based on the first letter of your last name. You may see a general advisor at the outset of your college years and later be assigned a subject-specific advisor for your major or program. If you get accepted into a specific program in your junior or senior year, the program head may be your advisor until graduation. This is often the case in health and medical programs.

You will typically be assigned an academic advisor after you have received your acceptance letter and informed the college that you plan to attend. It's possible that you have already met with an advisor during your campus orientation. Here are several important points to keep in mind for the advisement process.

It's critical that you understand how advisement is handled at the college or university you attend.

You may be required to first meet with your advisor after you've been accepted, but long before your first semester begins. It's possible you may be required to meet with your advisor for the first time a week before classes begin. In any event, *this is an important meeting*. Show up early, and wait if you have to. If you miss an appointment, you'll not only alienate your advisor, but you may not be able to get another appointment for weeks. I have been a faculty academic advisor for many years. I'm appalled at the number of students who don't value their advising appointments. I'd estimate that at least 50% of my advisees are late or don't show up. If you're late or absent for a second appointment, many advisors will tell you they won't see you again – get another advisor.

No matter who your advisor is, you need to show up to your appointments fully prepared.

Most advisees who come to my office are woefully unprepared. Don't plan on coming to advisement to be told what to do. Look over the program of study and course descriptions in detail before you go. The requirements for the academic programs at your college or university will be in a course catalog. Larger universities will have an enormous catalog, with every conceivable course under the sun. To save trees, you'll likely find it on the college's website.

You may hear the term "catalog rights." This means that you are bound only by the course and program requirements in the catalog of the year you begin school. We academics are always tinkering with the requirements of this major or that program. If you had to take new courses that were added to your major requirements or did not get credit for courses you took that were dropped as requirements, you'd never graduate. We certainly know this.

Have a written list of questions for your advisor. You may want to e-mail these to him or her in advance. When you make an appointment, be it via e-mail or over the phone, be sure to give your advisor your full name and student ID number so that it's easier for him or her to pull up your information. If your name has changed, through marriage or divorce, be sure to give your advisor both names. You should be encyclopedic about the courses you've taken, the ones you are currently enrolled in, and those you want to take, even though your advisor will have much of this information on the computer.

If you have changed your major or program, do not assume that the advisor you've been seeing is still your advisor.

After changing majors, ask admissions or the registrar if you've been assigned a new advisor. Many times I've had my advisees change majors and still come to me to get advised. When the appointment rolls around and I'm told of the change of plans, the new advisor he or she should be seeing is completely booked with appointments. Don't make the assumption that your advisor does advising for every program in the catalog.

Once you have chosen a major, met with an advisor, and know what classes you need to take and when, keep that program-of-study form like a love letter.

I still remember my undergraduate program-of-study form – two pages on green paper. I memorized it and referred to it constantly, not just before I registered each semester. I checked off the classes on those green sheets as I completed them and took notes for registration on them. They looked like guacamole by the time I graduated.

Your advisor is there to help you, but is not there to hold your hand.

Your advisor is the guardrail, but you are driving the car. You should be in control of your academic program after your first meeting or two with an advisor. Your advisor should be viewed as a safety net in case you've made a mistake, or if you need advice about electives or entrance requirements for specific programs. This came in handy when I was guilty of an oversight during my senior year. I was required to see my advisor a few semesters before graduation, just to make sure I had everything straight. As it turned out, I thought that a statistics course I completed would take the place of calculus as my math requirement. It didn't, but my advisor caught my mistake before it became a bigger issue.

If you've been away from school for many years and have decided to come back, you need to be keenly aware of how your previous coursework fits into your new academic plan.

There is no shame in coming back to school years after washing out. You would certainly not be the first to do so. Students lament this to me all the time. The story is usually a standard one. Your heart was not in academics when you first enrolled in college years ago. You majored in partying or you had an athletic scholarship and classes were an afterthought. You dropped more courses than you actually finished. The grades for the courses you finished were nothing to write home about. There was that semester when you finally hit rock bottom, dropped out and went home. You have four "F"s on your transcript to show for it.

This is where an advisor can certainly help. At some schools, you can set up an appointment with an advisor to sort out your previous academic shortcomings before you apply. This will give you an idea of what academic steps you need to take. Under the worst-case scenario, you may be required to retake what you failed and are granted only the option of averaging a new (hopefully better) grade with the old "D" or "F" for some courses. Sometimes you won't be required to average an old and new grade, but the old grade still factors into your GPA. Under the best-case scenario, you may be granted "amnesty," whereby you can start anew and those old grades are neither averaged in nor even kept on your transcript at all. In certain instances you can petition to have them removed from your transcript, even if you were initially told that they will remain. Follow the college's specific procedures for these processes. They will be found in the student handbook.

There is another potentially tough situation you might find yourself in. You may have earned stellar grades years before, but had to drop out due to financial problems or a personal issue. Fast-forward to the present, and the college won't accept those courses because they are "too old." This is another scenario whereby you may be able to petition to retain those credits. I was initially told that the statistics courses I took as part of my master's degree would not be accepted as part of my Ph.D. requirements, and that I'd have to retake those courses. I petitioned to get credit for them, pointing out that the courses I'd taken were 4-credit courses, while the ones I was being asked to take were 3-credit. I even kept the old syllabi, which verified that the courses I had taken went into greater detail than the new ones. It didn't hurt that I had made good grades in those courses, either. Eventually, the university gave me credit for the older courses.

That saved me dozens of classroom hours, hundreds of study hours, and a few thousand dollars.

Every college or university will have an "expiration date" for coursework. Some require courses older than ten years to be retaken, while some require only courses in your major, older than a certain number of years, to be retaken. A doctoral classmate of mine had fully completed his coursework for the degree but took too long to finish his dissertation and graduate. By the time he returned to complete the degree, seven courses he had successfully completed were too old and had to be retaken. I can't imagine taking seven courses over again that I'd successfully completed just a few years prior.

You may find that the college will accept many but not all of your older courses. If you took courses years or decades ago in a field that has changed significantly, like computers, you may be required to take those courses again. If you are applying for a nursing program, you may be required to take anatomy and physiology again.

2.3 Registration

The terms "advisement" and "registration" are often used synonymously. They are, however, two very different things. Advisement is when you are given advice about what courses to take and when. Registration is the physical act of signing up for those courses.

This is an area that has been completely transformed by technology. I registered for classes, in my first several semesters as an undergrad, using paper forms that had to be filled out and hand delivered to the registrar. A few semesters later, the university made registration available using a phone. Students were able to enter codes for each course over a landline. Next, students used a computer to register via a campus "intranet," although they had to go to a computer lab and use the university's computers. Now nearly all registration is done online, which you can do with your laptop from the beach. As with advisement, there are several issues associated with registration that require addressing.

Look over the master schedule in detail every time it comes out.

Colleges and universities will publish a master schedule of classes a few months before the next semester begins. Some will publish a master schedule for the upcoming two semesters. For decades, the master schedule was a booklet that the college piled in giant stacks in each building. Like the course catalog, it is now available online. By the time registration rolls around, you should have been advised and know the courses you need. As soon as the master schedule is available, use it to put together the schedule you want.

Do not forget to have a Plan B and Plan C schedule. This is the smart thing to do for many reasons. You may simply change your mind about classes as time passes. This is often the case when it comes to elective courses. Note that some courses are offered in only a spring or fall semester, only at night, or even only on Saturdays (gulp).

Sign up for classes at the first available time to get the courses you want and need.

Some institutions let everybody register at the same time. Others let seniors register first, then juniors and so on. Colleges I've taught at allowed those with the most credit hours taken at the college to register first, and those with fewer hours were allowed to register on successive days. Some institutions require you to be "unlocked" for registration by an advisor. That is, you cannot register for classes until you have seen your advisor and they've checked a box in your online profile that allows you to do so. Pay close attention to how your college has this arranged.

Popular classes fill up fast, as do specialized courses that may have only one section offered per semester or during the entire school year. Students often wonder why their college does not offer an unlimited number of sections if there are students who want or need them. There are many reasons for this, including limited facilities and a dearth of qualified professors.

Understand that the college has to cover its costs. If eight students are enrolled but it takes ten students to break even, the course may be cancelled. Most colleges will say that the course did not "make." Exceptions are sometimes made, especially if the few students enrolled need a course to graduate, but that is rare. *Have a backup plan in case this scenario occurs.* I've had to call a dozen students the day before classes started to tell them a course was cancelled and, needless to say, most were not happy. I can understand the frustration, but they rarely have a Plan B.

Register early to get the sections that fit into your personal schedule.

If you procrastinate with registration, the finance class you want to take may still have spaces available in a section or two, but that does you little good if you work during the times those sections are in session.

Some colleges allow late registration, often through the first week of class. *I do not suggest that you register for a class after it has started.* I cannot stress enough how important it is to attend the first day of class. You miss all of the important information the professor provides about the class if you register late. If you enroll after a full week, you may have already missed quizzes or other graded items. You will never fully get caught up. Over the years I have never seen a late registrant do well in a class – *ever*.

It's just the opposite. Those who are last to add the class are always the first to drop. I call this phenomenon "last in, first out." Admissions officers at colleges mistakenly think that this will give a last-minute bump to enrollment, but when these students inevitably realize they have made a mistake, they waste time at the registrar and financial aid offices, often get a refund, and end up costing the college time and money.

Some colleges will let you register even later than the first week, with the professor's permission. Students who approach me in these situations always say, "I know I can get caught up, Dr. Cubbage," or "I'll still do well in the class. You'll see." It never happens. Trust my experience – it simply is not in your best interest to add late.

Around the first week in April, you will tell yourself how much you are looking forward to a break from classes when spring semester is finished, but I strongly suggest taking at least one class each summer.

My occasional preaching may give you the impression that I was a buttoned-up college student who studied 24/7. Nothing is further from the truth. You bet I had fun in college. Nothing was more fun than college summers. The romanticism of the college summer is immortalized in dozens of movies, most recently in the American Pie series. However, you may find that college summers are not exactly what you thought they would be, nor are they like the movies.

I'll start with those of you who are going away to college and plan on returning home for your summers. *Don't take the summer off from schoolwork.* Knocking out some classes during summer will make your junior and senior years less hectic and stressful. The goal isn't necessarily a light academic load in those later years, but needing one or two fewer courses to graduate come your senior year will give you some breathing room. Consider taking some of the less-challenging courses over the summer. I don't want you to take any class lightly, but the fact is that some courses take more effort than others. Take summer classes, but give yourself a break from really intense coursework.

If at all possible, stay on campus for the summer. I know many things may prevent you from being able to do this. You may have an excellent summer job lined up back home. Perhaps your parents want you home for the summer. You may attend a college that does not offer summer classes and summer housing. If nothing is compelling you to come home, try to line up a summer job early in spring semester, enroll in a class or two, and enjoy all of the things that a less-crowded summer campus provides. You'll find that you can easily park around campus during summer. Campus offices are less crowded and the lines are shorter. I remember that the campus recreation center's basketball courts and swimming pool were almost too crowded to use during fall and spring, but I had the run of those facilities in summer. If you join a fraternity or sorority, you will love having the house mostly to yourself in summer.

Now I'll come back to what you might be expecting from your summers if you return home. It's possible that you return home and have a great summer reunion with your high school buddies. You'll pick up where you left off, compare notes about your freshman year, and have the time of your lives for the next three months. Don't count on it. I don't want to be a downer, but you may find that you've grown apart. In addition, you and your high school buddies will probably work during your summers and have little time to hang out.

If you do go home for summer, my advice about taking classes still stands. If there is another university or community college in your hometown, plan on taking at least one class there. Be sure to research the admissions requirements and semester dates to get administrative items taken care of well before summer classes begin. Don't wait until you are unpacking your car in your parents' driveway to get started. Many students at the community colleges where I've taught were home from universities for the summer, and were taking classes to transfer come fall.

Use summers to enhance your resumé and look better to potential employers down the road.

Taking classes in summer is helpful but, better yet, seek out internships, jobs or field courses in summer that relate to your major. Simply getting a degree in a certain field is no longer a guarantee that you'll get a job in your chosen field. A college roommate of mine worked summers for a large agricultural-equipment company. He had to spend those summers in another town, away from his buddies and girlfriend, but the job paid big bucks. He was hired full-time as soon as he graduated. He still works for that company twenty-five years later. A friend of mine takes students on a 4-credit field course to the Bahamas every summer to study ocean microbiology. Students get to spend the summer in an amazing environment and get valuable field experience.

Non-traditional and returning students benefit from summer schoolwork.

I know you "more seasoned" students are in a hurry to get on with your degree. Summer is an excellent way to do it. Take a full schedule if time and money will allow. In doing so, you can potentially finish your degree a semester or two early. I was an "older" student when I was earning my Ph.D. and wanted to progress quickly towards graduation. The university offered Summer 1 and Summer 2 sessions, which are back-to-back terms about a month long. I took classes in both sessions during two summers and it helped immeasurably. I was able to finish my Ph.D. much sooner as a result.

Chapter 3: Who's Teaching What? The Types Of Instructors You'll Encounter In College

You will encounter a wide variety of instructor titles throughout your college years. Instructors' names will come with an alphabet soup of different letters behind them. Who is teaching you or facilitating the class will depend on the size of your college, whether it's a public or private school, what year you are in school, the type of class you're taking, time of day you take classes, and a slew of other factors. Yet one thing is certain: your name is on the roster and the instructor's name is on the syllabus. That's a big distinction. Let's take a look at the most common types of instructors, their credentials, and what to expect from them.

3.1 Tenure-Track Professors

The archetype of an academic, also the most portrayed in pop culture, is the "tenured" or "tenure-track" professor. This conjures up images of the older, spectacled, grey-haired man in a tweed jacket. You may run across someone like this along the way, but that stereotype is not firmly tethered to reality. The career paths of professors in this category do contain some commonalities, though. The trek usually starts with earning a Ph.D. After that, he or she will sometimes complete a "post-doc" research project, with hopes of getting hired at a college or university. Once there, the goal is to earn tenure. That is, to complete a portfolio of research, teaching, and service over the course of a handful of years that will impress the institution enough to give him or her permanent employment. Along the way, one progresses from assistant professor to associate professor to the Holy Grail – full professor.

After they have earned tenure, professors will continue to conduct research in their fields and publish the results in scholarly journals and trade publications, as well as present research findings at conferences and symposia. Some are consultants for industry or expert witnesses in court proceedings. Many write college textbooks.

Professors wear many hats from day to day. They oversee graduate students completing master's and Ph.D. programs. Some may have a dozen or more graduate students at any one time. A tremendous amount of emphasis is placed on procuring grant money to fund their research. After all, the college gets a percentage of the funds that the professors rake in.

A tenured professor's teaching load varies, but it generally consists of a course or two per semester. This is a relatively low teaching load, but if your professor seems busy when you try to talk to him or her, bear in mind all of his or her aforementioned duties and responsibilities. If your professor is also in a leadership position, such as Department Chair or Dean, the teaching load may be reduced even further. At smaller colleges you may have all of your lower-level courses taught by tenure-track professors, but at larger schools you may not see many of them until you get to upper-level courses. You may have heard stories about the average tenure-track professor being consumed with research and eschewing the classroom, but this is largely untrue – most enjoy the classroom.

I didn't say that those who enjoy the classroom are all great teachers in the classroom. Being an expert in a subject and being able to communicate that expertise are two different things. Other than calculus, the course I stumbled through the most was organic chemistry. You'll have the joy of organic chemistry at some point if you're going into the sciences. The professor for my organic chemistry class had a last name that was sixteen letters long. I think I became confused by his name on the first day and never recovered. I took his class before PowerPoint and data projectors, so there were two overhead projectors (ask your parents) on either side of the stage that he projected onto a huge theater screen. He would write in red pen faster than he could talk, jumping back and forth between projectors and erasing as he went, making an already difficult subject completely inscrutable.

Yet he seemed to be having the time of his life. A fellow student said the professor was always smiling because he reveled in thinking, "Look what I know that you don't." Despite examples like this, you'll find that most professors are proficient at teaching and excel in the classroom. You have much to learn from them. In particular, the faculty I had for my Ph.D. coursework were all amazingly gifted in the classroom and are, in large part, the inspiration for how I approach my teaching to this day. My Ph.D. dissertation committee chair and mentor, who was also my professor for several classes, won several prestigious teaching awards.

3.2 Non-Tenure-Track Professors

You will also have many non-tenure instructors, even at top-tier universities. Much of the faculty at many smaller colleges, and at most community colleges, have master's degrees in their subjects. Their titles will vary as a result, but many institutions with unionized faculty will confer the generic title of professor on people in this category. They may also be able to earn some form of tenure, although it is optional.

Don't underestimate this type of professor. Most of them do not conduct research, have graduate students, or chase grant money. Rather, they are professional teachers who may teach five or more sections per semester. Some tenure-track professors teach a particular course once per year, while a non-tenure-track instructor may teach ten or more sections a year of the same course. As a result, they can be exceptionally good at teaching each specific course in their repertoire. A similar position often found at larger universities is that of "master teacher," although you may see slightly different titles in this case. These are teachers of a particular subject who teach full time and generally do not conduct research. They may have a Ph.D. or master's degree, but there is no opportunity for tenure.

3.3 Adjunct Professors

Up to this point, the instructors I've discussed are almost exclusively full-time employees at their respective schools, but colleges and universities of all types rely heavily on part-time instructors these days, usually referred to as "adjunct" instructors. At many schools, upwards of 50% of all classes are taught by adjuncts. It's simple economics. It costs much less to employ a handful of adjuncts than to hire a full-time instructor. Most of them receive few employee benefits from the institution. You might be wondering why tuition costs so much if so many cheaper adjuncts are teaching. That's a great question, but is out of the scope of this book (hint: ask the administrators where you have enrolled, as there are more than enough of them these days to answer that question). Adjuncts typically sign a new teaching contract each semester, and have no guarantee of longer-term employment. In some states, adjunct instructors are trying to unionize.

I hired all of the adjuncts in my department for a decade, and they all reported to me. During those years, probably 90% of the student issues I dealt with were from my adjuncts' students. This was no reflection on the adjuncts' talent, performance, or professionalism. It was due to the most dubious of reasons – students somehow figured out who the adjuncts were, often thought less of them, and tried to get away with more in their classes.

This is incredibly unfortunate, because adjuncts are some of the best teachers you'll have in college. Several adjuncts I hired taught for me for many years, had great reputations, and were among the most popular instructors. They are to be treated with the same respect as any instructor with a fancier title. Many are working full-time in their subject and bring real-world experience to the classroom. Many teach a couple of classes each semester at more than one institution, and thus have the equivalent of a full-time teaching load.

Some adjuncts teach during the day, but if you sign up for a night class, chances are that the instructor will be an adjunct. Most of the full-time faculty are long gone by 6:00 p.m. (if not 3:00 p.m.). The same is often the case in summer, when many full-time faculty take the summer off and the college has to rely more heavily on adjuncts. When people find out I'm a college professor they always ask me if I get summers off. I tell them I can't take the summer off until the mortgage lender gives me the summer off. It would be fabulous if the mail carrier stopped putting bills in the mailbox during summer, but I'm not holding my breath.

I started my career in higher education as an adjunct. I had a full-time job as an environmental consultant during the day and taught Biology 101 at night. I didn't need the money at the time. Like so many other adjuncts, I was teaching for the most noble of reasons – I just loved the classroom. It was a tremendous experience, and it validated that teaching was my calling. Without my experience as an adjunct it's unlikely I would have been hired full-time. Many professors started out this way. I continued to take adjunct jobs at different institutions after becoming a full-time professor to broaden my horizons and teach a wider variety of courses.

3.4 Teaching Assistants

Lower-level undergraduate courses and lab components of many courses are often taught by a teaching assistant, or "TA." A TA is usually a graduate student who assumes teaching responsibilities in return for free tuition and a stipend or fellowship. A TA has a bachelor's and sometimes a master's degree. It's surprising how good TAs typically are, considering that most are new to teaching and get precious little training for the classroom.

On balance, the TAs I had when I was a student were excellent instructors who were enthusiastic in the classroom. I had four semesters of German as an undergrad, and all of them were taught by TAs. Nearly all of my biology labs were taught by TAs, as were some of my general-education lecture courses. Many TAs are also graders for larger classes. In those instances a professor teaches the class, but TAs proctor on exam days and do the grading. A few of my finals were in large amphitheaters with all of the students from the other sections of the course that semester, and TAs proctored them.

I was a research assistant when I was a master's student, but I also filled in occasionally in the classroom if one of the professors or TAs was sick or out of town. I was asked to give a guest lecture on my research project a few times. You may have senior undergraduates help out in certain classes or teaching labs. They also work sometimes as tutors.

3.5 Other Considerations With Regard To Your Professors

You will also have a diversity of professors in college by gender, ethnicity, age and so forth. As for gender, women have made tremendous strides in higher education over the last few decades and have subsequently increased their numbers on college faculties. It's a safe bet that you'll have twice as many female professors as I did in the 1980s.

The numbers of foreign-born instructors has greatly increased as well. At one point I had instructors on my staff from Australia, India, Cameroon and Taiwan. From time to time you may have an instructor from overseas who has a thick accent. Resist the temptation to be critical or to blame your struggles on his or her English. Instead of being snarky, the best thing you can do is to appreciate the fact that he or she had the fortitude to earn an advanced degree in a second language. Most people say that public speaking terrifies them more than anything. Imagine public speaking in a foreign country. It takes courage to get in front of a classroom full of students who don't speak your native language. Consider also that your instructor's English is probably much better than your Hindi or Mandarin.

Get to know your foreign instructors and ask them questions about their native cultures. I guarantee you'll find it fascinating, and it may inspire you to study abroad. I love having international students in my classes, and I am at rapt attention when they talk about their homelands and the journeys they took to get to the United States. They are typically excellent students, and often spell better in English than many students born in this country. One of the best writers I ever had in my classes was a twenty-year-old woman from Ukraine who started learning English at the age of seventeen.

The next topic requires a trip into the world of sports. You may have heard of the legendary basketball coach Bobby Knight. He led the Indiana University basketball team to national championships and even an undefeated season. He is also legendary for less admirable behavior, including throwing a chair onto the court during a game, head butting a player, and saying just about anything that came to mind, inappropriate or not. Whether you loved him or hated him, his teams were winners.

Coach Knight also taught a class in Coaching of Basketball. He was as tough on his students as he was on his players. Coach Knight spoke in no apologies about how intensely he challenged his students. He was not a "player's coach," one who asks little of his or her players and demands only a modicum of discipline. Likewise, he wasn't a "student's teacher" in the classroom. I've always said that there is a place for player's coaches – second place. Coach Knight had a saying as well. To paraphrase, write down the three hardest teachers you ever had. Then write down the three best teachers you ever had. If you were any student at all, the names on both lists should be the same.

When I was in college I became involved in coaching of youth sports, mainly soccer, in the local park-and-recreation leagues. It was a welcome break from my studies, and it honed my motivational and teaching skills. Things went well, and I was asked to be an assistant coach on a traveling team. The head coach, Coach Hampson, was an older Englishman. He was a local legend: proper, intense, and highly structured. If one of the kids wasn't pulling his weight or performing the way he should, he could expect an earful, whether he was right next to Coach Hampson or all the way across the field. For the younger readers of this book, most of the coaches in your parents' or grandparents' day were like this. If you're under thirty, you may have never had a coach holler at you. Coach Hampson's approach was going out of style, but the parents didn't say much about it because his teams won. It's funny how that works.

Our coaching styles were complementary and meshed well. It was good cop/bad cop. Coach Hampson would tear them down with his criticism and I would build them back up with soft encouragement. We were winning every tournament we entered, many of which had dozens of teams in our division from several states. We had talent at every position and talent on the bench – every coach's dream.

Near the end of the season, Coach Hampson went out of town for work and left the team in my hands. What happened next was jarring. I couldn't control the kids during practice. They ignored my commands and talked back. They slacked and messed around. With me at the helm, we had our first loss of the season at the outset of the next tournament and found ourselves in the loser's bracket. It was a tough road to claw back into contention. I lay in bed that night searching for answers, and finally it dawned on me. They *liked* me, but they *respected* Coach Hampson. He was "hard," but they responded to it. I was easygoing and lenient, which was the worst approach I could have taken.

You will hear all sorts of rumors about certain professors on campus. There will be an undercurrent about who is "hard" and who is "easy." I hate to use those terms, but for lack of better ones I'll stick with them for the sake of this discussion. There are all sorts of websites where students can go to read about what professors are hard or easy. This professor is an easier grader than the others, professor X requires more papers than professor Y, this professor's tests are too hard or that professor does not "give anybody an 'A' in her classes." I heard this talk from some of the students when I was in school. They were always the worst students.

Without exception, don't run away from the "hard" instructors' courses – *run to them!* You may have to study a bit more or see more red on your graded papers, but you will be richly rewarded. They will get the most out of you. They will prepare you for higher-level courses and graduate school. You'll probably earn an "A" because you are seriously into the class.

I get letters and e-mails from former students all the time that say things such as, "I thought you were too hard at the time, but without you I would have not gotten into nursing school." I keep them in what I call my "bad day box." When I'm having a bad day, I get that box out and read some of those letters. I wish I had sent the same types of letters to those hard professors who made such a difference in my life. Indeed, the three best teachers I ever had were the three hardest teachers, and I'll always be in their debt because of it. I want the same for you.

Keep in mind that the teaching profession at the college level is no different from any other walk of life – it's composed of human beings. I've been positive about what most college instructors bring to the table, and nearly all of them whose courses you take will be good at what they do. But just as most plumbers or engineers or physicians and the like are good at what they do, some of them are mediocre and a few inevitably are, well, bad. The professorship is no different. I have reluctantly had to let a few instructors go over the years because they were just not working out, even with my help and support. I feel bad for the students who took those instructors during their brief attempts at teaching, but that's life.

Another phenomenon you might experience is the new instructor. Community colleges are great places for those interested in college teaching to get a start. I always endeavored to provide ample mentoring to the green professors. Most became solid instructors, but it took time to get there. There is no crime in that. Any instructor, whether a tenured, full professor or a TA just a few years older than you, had to teach for the first time at some point.

I always admonish first-time instructors to keep that fact from the class. I've had plenty of students in my office over the years who chose to come and complain because they were earning a bad grade and found out they had a first-time instructor. When I dug a bit deeper they always admitted that they weren't studying enough, hadn't bought the book, missed some class or were chronically tardy. I would ask them also why they waited until the day they found out the instructor was new to come and complain.

Professors have different personalities. Some are effervescent while others are icy. Some are hysterically funny while some are dreadfully boring. One of my colleagues approaches her lectures like a one-woman show on Broadway. She jumps up and down, makes points with corny but cute analogies, and acts out biological processes with the physical comedy of Jim Carrey or Will Ferrell. Students take her course first in a two-semester sequence and then take me for the second course. They seem surprised when I don't burst out into song. I tell them not to mistake a laid-back personality for a lack of enthusiasm. I'm enjoying myself just as much as she is. Our personalities are just different. (And you really don't want to hear me sing.) The working world, after graduation, will be no different. You will spend a lifetime juggling co-workers' and subordinates' personalities, while having to accept those of your bosses.

You might be tempted to ascribe a bad grade in a class to a mediocre or inexperienced instructor, but you should resist that entirely. A professor may have been a jerk, a bad communicator, or just plain lazy, but you still had the textbook, online resources, tutoring, and all manner of other resources to get you through. Get accustomed to just sucking it up and dealing with it. *Ultimately, you are responsible for your learning and have ownership over your grade.*

Chapter 4: The Same Pie With Different Recipes: Types Of Class Formats

As part of your college experience, professors don't just want to teach you *what* to think, but *how* to think. To know how to think, you must first master how to learn. There are as many ways to learn as there are different subjects to learn.

Thus, some courses will have a small number of seats available, while others will essentially be unlimited. You will get to know every fellow student in some classes. In other classes you may never meet another student. Some classes will require you to be in class at a specific time, while others will allow you to log on virtually to a class at your leisure.

You will have many class formats to choose from over your college years. The options have grown and evolved significantly over the last few decades. The format and learning environment for many of your classes are tremendously different than those your parents experienced during their college years. Here are the major types of class formats you'll find when you get to campus, and how to navigate them.

4.1 Traditional Lecture Courses

Despite the explosive growth in the variety of ways many classes are delivered, traditional lecture classes are still common. This age-old concept is often known as the "sage on the stage." The professor stands in front of the class and lectures about the course material. Traditional lectures vary wildly in enrollment size. You may show up to class on the first day and have just a dozen fellow students, sometimes fewer. Then again, you may be in a class with hundreds of your "closest friends." As a general rule, the largest classes are freshman lecture classes and "core" classes that most students are required to take.

The type of college you attend factors into this. If you attend a small, liberal arts college, you may never have a class with more than thirty students in it. At large research universities you may have three hundred students in a lecture. I started college at a small, liberal arts institution in the Midwest. My largest lecture class had about thirty-five students. When I transferred to a huge Big Ten school, I took some classes in the same auditorium where I attended rock concerts. Either way, the professor did the talking and we did the listening.

That's not to say that professors do not ask the class questions or do not want to field them. Although I adamantly discourage in-class questions about things you can find in the syllabus or personal questions that apply only to you, *I strongly encourage you to ask content-related questions during your classes*. This not only helps you understand material you may be struggling with – it shows that you are engaged and interested in what's going on. Don't rudely interrupt, and don't tell the professor that he or she is going too fast. Do, however, raise your hand until you're called on. You'd be surprised how many of your classmates have the same question you do.

In terms of facilities, traditional lecture courses may take place in classrooms that look exactly like those from high school. They may be scheduled in large lecture rooms with stadium seating. This hasn't changed much over the years. Note that many of the older lecture halls I took classes in had ashtrays on every chair! Believe it or not, smoking was commonplace in classrooms for decades. I had one or two professors who still smoked in class, although that practice was dying quickly.

What has changed dramatically is the manner in which the lecture material is presented. During my first few years in college, most professors used an old-school chalkboard. That was replaced by the overhead projector. The overhead projector overlapped with the new "whiteboard." The whiteboard is now a "Smart Board," and the overhead projector was retired when data projectors hit the scene.

You may still take professors who use an old whiteboard, but *be prepared to adapt to any new technology that is used in class.* Before long, we will likely be using hologram and 4-D technology as lecture-delivery methods. I use technology in my classroom and encourage my colleagues to do the same, as long as it genuinely enhances the learning experience. You may see technology misapplied here and there. It might look cool but not fit the lesson. Hopefully, any technology you are exposed to will genuinely enhance your learning.

4.2 Small-Group Discussion Courses

As you move up to your junior and senior years, you may take courses that are rooted in student discussion. If you go to graduate school, all or most of your coursework will be in this format. It is often used in the humanities, social sciences, and fine arts. You might sit in a circle and discuss your ideas, opinions, and analyses regarding class topics. If you've written a research paper, you may be asked to give an overview of your findings and answer questions about them.

The professor's role in these courses varies. He or she may take a leading role in the discussions. In other classes, the professor might present topics and act as a facilitator, but let the students do most of the talking. You may be assigned to lead the discussion on a particular day. Small-group discussion courses are my favorite to teach. I always learn as much from the students as they learn from me.

An offshoot of this delivery method involves the professor lecturing and then opening up the floor to discuss what was presented. This is often the case in language classes. I had several German courses that were taught this way. Any student in those courses who did not voluntarily participate in the discussion would eventually be called on to participate. Having a hangover was no excuse to detach from the ongoing class. This wasn't the professor or TA being a sadist. The point was to get everybody meshed into the material each class day, which is the best way to learn a language.

4.3 Laboratory Courses

Nearly every science course has a laboratory component with it. Some colleges combine the lecture and lab components into one course, while others have the lecture and lab as separate but related courses. Labs are not exclusive to science courses. Computer, math, and even music courses may have components that fall under the lab umbrella. The professor from lecture may teach the lab, or a TA or student worker might teach it. You'll probably have to purchase a separate book, usually referred to as a "lab manual."

The instructor for your section of a lab course may run the lab differently than another instructor does in teaching a section of the same lab course. Your syllabus for lecture may spell out all the aspects of the lab (e.g. schedule, grading) or you may receive a separate syllabus for lab. In a traditional, on-campus lab, you will do experiments and other hands-on exercises that are related to the lecture or text material you're covering. This may be right after lecture or on a completely different day than lecture.

A typical lab runs longer than a typical lecture, as more time is needed for setup, experimentation, and cleanup. You may be required to complete lab exercises on your own, but more than likely you'll have a lab partner or be part of a lab group. Some lab courses require you to keep a lab notebook that is periodically turned in for grading, and you may have a quiz before or after each lab exercise.

My biology lab courses, and most science lab courses, have two or three "lab practical exams," or "practicals." Practicals are composed of several stations with displays from the material we have covered, and each station has a couple of questions. Students get a few minutes at each station. For example, I may have microscopes out with slides already set up, and the questions might be as follows:

"What cell type is at the end of the pointer?"

"What hormone does this cell type produce?"

In some lab practical exams, all of the material will be set up and students are just required to answer questions. Other practicals require students to perform tasks under the eye of the professor, who grades them on how well they perform the techniques.

Labs may be held outdoors. Obviously it makes sense to have some biology labs outside, and even engineering or architecture classes might have field labs. One of my favorite labs during my college years was the lab for a "limnology" course. That's the study of freshwater lakes, rivers and streams – not lemons. (My girlfriend at the time thought I was taking a class on citrus.) At any rate, the lab lasted an entire day each week. We traveled in university vans to various locations and performed field experiments. Then we took samples back to the lab, performed lab analyses, and completed lab reports. We fostered a class camaraderie like none other I experienced in college. It was a total blast, and a great break from sitting in a traditional classroom.

I took a class in graduate school in wildlife diseases that had a lengthy lab. We all brought in roadkill to necropsy (dissect) in the lab, and we had a bet going about who could bring in the most obscure species. It was a tie between a dead great horned owl I found in my backyard and a bobcat another student found dead on the side of the road. I loved that lab, with the exception of the time I almost cut off my finger with a scalpel while cutting open a dead beaver (see safety admonishment below). I still have the scar from that episode.

Here is a list of helpful hints to maximize the lab experience:

- Never be late for a lab. Nothing is worse for you – or more distracting to your fellow lab students – than you walking in when lab exercises are already in progress. Pull your weight in lab and don't expect your lab partner to do everything.
- Read over the exercises before going to lab. Don't walk into lab without a clue what the exercises are going to be. Lab will go much smoother when you are prepared for what you're going to be doing. If there is an optional lab simulation you can do online before lab, by all means do it.
- Arrive with everything you need. You might survive a lecture if you forget your notebook, but you may not have the capability to complete the lab exercises if you leave something important at home. In microbiology lab you're

turned away if you show up with open-toed shoes and/or without your lab coat.

- Always, always, always follow all lab safety policies and procedures (especially while slicing open dead beavers). You will be shown the locations of eye-wash stations, spill kits, fire extinguishers, safety glasses, and the like on the first day. If for some reason you do have an injury, no matter how small, tend to it immediately according to proper procedures and notify the instructor.

- Most labs, especially science labs, do not allow food or drink. Leave your sodas and chips at home. This is for your own safety. You will be handling items that have been touched by hundreds of students that week, many of whom may have been sick. Do you really want to touch your hands to your mouth?

- Tell the instructor at the beginning of the semester if you have any health issues that might be compromised or exacerbated by any of the lab activities planned for the term. As per the Health Insurance Portability and Accountability ACT (HIPPA) you do not have to give any details, but the instructor has no way of knowing about your personal circumstances unless you inform him or her. For more information on HIPPA, please visit www.hhs.gov/ocr/privacy.

- The best way to get the most out of lab is to do well in the lecture portion of the course. Lab just brings lecture to life. If you have mastered the text material, you will understand why you are doing specific lab exercises, and you will see the relationships between the two course components.

4.4 Hybrid Courses

By definition, a hybrid anything is made up of two (or maybe more) different things. A hybrid course fits this definition because it consists of two different delivery methods that are designed to complement each other.

Although most hybrid courses include an online component, not all hybrid courses are the same. In my hybrid courses, the "lecture" or "textbook" material is presented online. There are online lectures and video clips, links to content-related websites, and other learning tools that I have organized. The students can access those materials, and complete online assignments at any time of the day or night, as long as they submit the material before stated deadlines. The students have to come to campus for the lab portion of my hybrid courses. I make time at the outset of lab to answer questions about the text material, but the class period is devoted to lab activities.

Some of my colleagues teach hybrid math courses that require students to complete online problem sets and watch video lectures. The class meets on campus once a week, where the professor lectures about the class topics. Quizzes are taken online, but all exams must be taken in class. Other colleagues of mine teach hybrid computer courses. Students learn theory and complete assignments online, but they must come to a computer lab to apply what they have learned. In some sections of those courses, the students are assigned a specific lab day and time. Labs for some hybrid courses may be scheduled for specific dates and times, or students may be able to attend "open labs" at their convenience.

You gain a great deal of *flexibility* when you take a hybrid section, but you assume a great deal of *responsibility*. If you are working, have a family, and/or are taking a large course load, a hybrid section cuts down on the time you have to physically be in class.

By the same token, it's your responsibility to be disciplined and to complete the online portion of the course in a timely manner.

I stress to my hybrid-course students that, although they have to be present only once a week, they should not dedicate only that one day each week to the class. Students tend to think that, because their hybrid class meets on Tuesday, the only day they need to work on the class is Tuesday. *Just as you should do for any traditional class, spend time each day studying for a hybrid class.* Similarly, there is no excuse for being tardy in a hybrid class. If you only have to be in class once a week, it's not unreasonable to request that you be on time.

4.5 Fully Online Courses

Of all the new class-delivery methods that technology has brought us, this is by far the most revolutionary. An entire industry based exclusively on online learning has sprouted up. Twenty-five years ago it was unimaginable that students would be able to sit at their home computers, or at a café with their laptops, and take college courses – without ever stepping into a classroom.

When I was an undergrad, the college I attended had one of the first major "intranets" in higher education. My roommate had a dial-up modem (I can still remember the sound) that we used for logging into the campus intranet to do lab simulations. It seems like Pong now compared to just my first cell phone, let alone the internet.

On a broader scale, many for-profit institutions offer online classes only. Some traditional brick-and-mortar colleges and universities have developed fully online degrees as well. If you are living on campus, you may be limited to a certain number of online courses you can take in a given semester, or over the course of your entire degree.   The college wants you to interact in person with professors and fellow students.

You may have received a taste of online learning in high school. Many high schools have online offerings, and homeschooled students have access to complete high school curricula online. Even so, you need to be familiar with the online modes of teaching and learning used at your institution.   It's critical that you are familiar with success strategies for online learning prior to ever enrolling in an online course. Waiting until you've enrolled in an online class to get familiar with your college's online learning tools or, even worse, after an online class has started, is a recipe for disaster.

I do not recommend that you enroll in an online (or hybrid) course if you are not extremely proficient with computers, and online computing in particular, especially downloading and uploading files. *Online courses are designed for those who already possess those skills; they are not designed to teach them.* Most colleges have an online tutorial that helps you learn how to use their online course platform, and you may be able to schedule a session with somebody from the college's computer-support department to help you as well. Sitting down at a computer with a fellow student who is well versed in online learning can help you brush up on the necessary computer skills.

These insights will help you decide if you are ready to take an online course.   In today's technology-driven environment, it is highly unlikely that you'll have no online learning responsibilities in your college years and beyond. There is one major caveat: once you have acquired those skills, *I still do not suggest taking a subject online that you are weak in.*

For example, if you have done well in English over the years, by all means consider taking an online English course if it gives you more schedule flexibility, but if you have struggled in science, do not enroll in an online biology, physics or chemistry course. What I often see is that the "A" students, who would thrive in an online course and benefit immensely from the flexibility, think that they'd stumble and don't enroll in it. Conversely, the weaker students wait too late to register and the only thing open at that point is the online section. Both types of students just end up hurting themselves.

Online classes are for self-starting, resourceful students. Nobody will be there to make sure you've completed your work. Your professor won't be in your dorm room or basement looking over your shoulder. If you need to be constantly reminded about completing your work on time, you're probably not doing well in the online format. *It bears repeating – when you take an online course, you have gained flexibility but assumed more responsibility.*

If you do go the online route, online learning starts with accessing your college's platform for online learning. This is essentially a website for your online classes. The most common, copyrighted platforms are Blackboard, Canvas, and D2L, but there are others. All of them have the same basic elements. You log on to the online platform web address you should have been given when you enrolled at the college, and there should also be a link through the college's web page (sometimes even the specific department's web page). Your college-assigned username and password are often the same ones you use to log in for online learning.

Log in, well before you enroll in a specific online course, just to make sure you can do it. You may be prompted to change your password from the one the college assigned you, and passwords expire every six months or so. You can expect an e-mail to your campus e-mail inbox reminding you of the date when your password expires. Don't procrastinate in changing your password. There is nothing more maddening than having your password expire on the day of an online exam.

When you log in to the college's website you will likely see links to all of the courses you have enrolled in, whether they are online or not. Even traditional lecture sections have an online page these days. If you click on your online course link, you should be directed to the course's landing page. If you pan across the landing page you will see all manner of links, but don't be intimidated.

The first thing that should jump out at you is the announcements. Think of the announcements as a combination vacation itinerary, assembly directions, and the kiosk at the mall that tells you where everything is, all rolled up into one. This is where the professor posts what the latest assignments are, due dates, subjects currently being covered, and anything else he or she thinks you need to be apprised of.

Even though it's unlikely that there will be new announcements every day, you need to check for them every day. Some online platforms even have inexpensive apps for smartphones and tablets. Most of us look at our smartphones dozens or even hundreds of times a day. You can use one of those times to log on and check for course-related announcements. I have my course announcements sent to my students' campus e-mail addresses, but I still insist that they log in every day. If you go several days without logging in, you will undoubtedly miss important information.

Please read the announcements carefully. If you take an online course, it is your responsibility to do so. Take a screen shot if it will help you remember important information. I can't tell you how many times students have e-mailed me asking for information that was presented in an online announcement. My response is always, "Please read the announcements, which answer your question."

Online assignments, learning tools, and associated responsibilities come in many forms. Some are generic and can be found in any online course for just about any subject, and some are specific to particular subjects. Here are some common components of the online class experience, with suggestions about how to make the most of them.

Online quizzes and exams.

Any major online course platform allows the professor to build and post quizzes and exams that students can take online. An announcement usually accompanies any quiz or exam. It will tell you how many hours or days you have to log in and take the quiz or test. For example, an announcement might read as follows:

"Greetings, students. The Chapter 8 quiz will be available under the Quizzes link from noon on Sunday through noon on Tuesday."

Too many students see this as an opportunity to wait until 11:30 a.m. on Tuesday to log in and take the exam. The professor doesn't have to punish you for waiting – life will take care of that. Your virus scan will kick on and log you off, your kid will fall and get hurt or any one of a thousand other distractions will happen. Murphy's Law was practically invented for computers and online work.

Those who wait until the last minute to get logged in and take a quiz or exam are invariably the weaker students. Almost without fail, the "A" students take the exam when it first becomes available. *Do not wait until the last minute to log on and take online quizzes and exams.* You give yourself no wiggle room if you experience problems.

When I post a quiz or exam, it is my expectation that the students have completed their studying and are ready to take it. An announcement about a quiz or exam is not a prompt to *begin* studying for it. In some instances you may be required to complete a series of online assignments before you can open the quiz or exam link.

This brings us to the actual act of taking the quiz or exam. Always treat an online quiz or exam as if you were physically in class to take it. Make sure everybody else is out of your apartment or house so that they won't interrupt you. Leave your books and other class materials in another room so that you won't be tempted to cheat. *Never forget that online cheating is still cheating.* Some computer systems record video of you taking the exam to verify that you didn't cheat.

Don't log in to take the exam when there is bad weather and your connection may be lost. I know you have the Weather Channel. Use the computer and internet service you have always used if it has been reliable. Using a computer you are unfamiliar with just invites problems, such as a cursor mistake. Taking a quiz or exam in a new location will interfere with your focus, and you may hit the wrong key or button by accident. How many times have you used a new device and fumbled around with the unfamiliar key placements?

Understand that your professor is not responsible for your computer issues. He or she may have 100 students in an online section, all of whom have different devices, internet providers/Wi-Fi, browsers, and so forth. The good news is that online course platforms have become more reliable in recent years, and glitches are less frequent. There is still the occasional desperate student e-mail exclaiming that, "I logged on to take the quiz and it kicked me off." Each professor's policy in this situation is different, but one thing is the same – *we don't like getting these e-mails*.

When you click on the directed link such as "Tests" or "Quizzes," you will see the icon for the quiz or exam you are about to take. When you click on this icon you will typically be prompted to verify that you want to start, and you will see information and instructions, including how long you have to take the quiz or exam, the number of questions, the format for the questions, and the total number of possible points.

Once you begin, a timer should be visible somewhere on the screen. Scroll down through the entire quiz or exam so that you can get familiar with it. Then, just as with any quiz or exam, answer the questions you are certain about first. Most of my online quizzes and exams are a mixture of true/false and multiple-choice questions, but professors may also use matching, short answer or any number of other question formats.

Do not linger in the quiz or exam. I'm not suggesting that you rush unnecessarily, but the longer you have it open, the more things there are that can go wrong. The fewer clicks you make, the better. If you have the option to save your answers, by all means do it, but I always say, "Get in and get out." I have never magically come up with all of the answers in the last minute of a quiz or exam, and you won't either – nobody does.

Every professor has different rubrics for grading quizzes and exams, as well as a policy about how many attempts you may have. Most of the time you just get one chance. Other times you may get two or three chances to take the test, or you may take it as many times as it takes until you pass. Some professors let you take online quizzes several times, but take the online exams only once. This information should be stated in the syllabus.

The beauty of online exams is that, unless short-answer or essay questions have to be hand-graded, you know immediately how you scored, which greatly cuts down on grading errors. Sometimes you will be able to see your raw score only, but the professor has the option of letting you see what questions you missed, what the correct answers were, and feedback about the correct answers.

Don't hound the professor if he or she does not give you all of this information. Professors can't reuse a quiz or exam if they have allowed students to print it out or take a screen shot of it. I try to have several versions of every quiz or exam, which I rotate and update each semester, but I don't always have time to do this. All of my online students might not live near campus, but I give them the opportunity to come in during office hours and go over the entire quiz or exam with me.

Final exams for online classes almost always have to be taken in person. If you live on or near the campus that offers the online class, you may be given several options for days and times to come in and take the final. This is to discourage cheating throughout the semester. Don't be tempted to ask your uncle who works for NASA to do your work for you in your online astronomy class. It will be you sitting there for the final, and you'll have to show identification (usually your student ID card).

Some students live hundreds or thousands of miles away from the home campus while they are enrolled in an online class. In those instances they can take the final at an approved testing location, such as another college near their home. For verification purposes, your professor will need to know the proctor's name, location and title. It is your responsibility to get everything organized and scheduled. When the proctor is verified, the professor will e-mail him or her information about the exam and the exam itself. The proctor will then send the completed exam back via e-mail or even snail mail (postal service).

Message and discussion threads.

Polishing interpersonal communication skills is an important part of your overall college experience. Taking an online class denies you this face-to-face interaction. To remedy this, most online courses provide an opportunity for you to interact with your classmates in the form of online discussions on message boards. It's no different than blogging. The professor may give the class a topic and require the students to discuss and debate it online. How much the professor requires you to do varies. In some of my online classes (and hybrids) I post anywhere from one to three topics per week. These are usually referred to as "forums."

At a minimum, my students are required to start their own discussion on each topic and respond in another student's discussion. I try to stay away from the word "minimum" when I'm constructing assignments but find it almost impossible to do so. Most professors will tell you that when they say something is the minimum, that's all that most students do. Sometimes it's like pulling teeth to get my undergrads to make the most of online discussions. In contrast, the discussions explode in my graduate-level classes. Right off the bat there might be fifty or seventy-five posts in a class with fifteen students. Immerse yourself in the online discussions. If you just do the minimum, you may be *participating* in the discussions, but you're not *contributing* anything to them.

There is often a deadline for posting discussions, and the message board will go away at that time. *As with online quizzes and tests, do not wait until the last minute to start posting in an online message board.* If you do that, you give your classmates no time to read and respond to your posts. You also cannot read your classmates' posts, and *you should read every post.* Log in every day and you won't have to read all of them at the last minute. You'll be surprised how insightful some of your classmates can be. The professor may break you up into groups for online discussions. If you don't participate, it may affect your classmates' grades on the assignment.

There are rules of etiquette when posting to online discussions. Blogs almost always degenerate into ugly, petty arguing. This gives way to juvenile name-calling and before you know it, the bloggers aren't even discussing the topic anymore. You may have noticed this in blogs or been guilty of this behavior yourself at some point, but it won't be tolerated in the higher-education setting. No matter how passionate you are about a topic, and no matter how wrong you think one of your classmates might be, compose your online discussions as if you are sitting next to each other actually talking. Be respectful and professional. Never make it personal.

That's not to say you should avoid saying what you really want to say. Without honesty, online discussions would be meaningless. An open exchange of ideas is what college is all about (or at least it once was, and should still be). Don't be afraid to make a counterpoint or highlight a flaw in a classmate's analysis. *Try to back up your points with references, which you should include at the bottom of your posts.* Use proper English and stick to the point. Avoid slang and anything that might come across as an indication of anger (e.g. using all caps).

Online lectures and online video clips.

Something I hear all the time is, "I don't want to take an online class. I need a lecture." All online courses are a bit different, but most have some sort of lecture video material on the course topics.

Professors can do "lecture capture," where they record themselves lecturing in traditional fashion and post those lectures to the class's site. Be thankful for this convenience. I took a class as part of my Ph.D. that required us to check out a long series of DVDs. I was stuck sitting next to a television for a semester. I distinctly remember watching those DVDs on a TV in our beach condo. Not only was everybody else at the beach while I was parked on the couch, but the DVD player was ancient, and it skipped whenever the professor made an important point. I'm sure that class and the related materials are online now.

Two words you will see related to online lectures are "synchronous" and "asynchronous." Synchronous means "at the same time." In this case, you may have to be at your computer or have your device out at a specific day and time for a lecture that the professor is streaming live. Depending on the technology, you may be able to ask questions and interact with classmates during the lecture. "Asynchronous" means "at different times." These lectures have been pre-recorded and posted to your class website. You can log on in your pajamas at 3:00 a.m. and watch them. You can pause them, rewind them, skip over part of them, and so forth.

You may see these terms used for lectures in hybrid classes as well. I taught a hybrid class that had a synchronous lecture each week, but the rest of the course consisted of online, asynchronous exercises. Message boards and online discussions may also be synchronous or asynchronous.

In addition to video lectures, online courses may have smaller video clips for you to watch. Some classes may have full-length lectures over an entire chapter and shorter video pieces on the individual topics from that lecture. Links may be posted that send you out to the internet for more video.

None of this stops you from finding additional study materials on the internet on your own. *Never confine yourself to what the professor has given you to study with, online or otherwise.* The resources you have online were unimaginable just a generation ago. There is no excuse for not using them. One three-minute video clip you find on the internet may clarify what your professor was trying to tell you over the course of an hour in class. I tell my biology students that I would have given my right arm when I was an undergrad just for Google images, let alone the rest of the internet! Almost every slide, plastic model, and piece of equipment in my biology labs can be found on Google images.

Virtual and self-directed labs.

If you take an online course with a lab component, expect to do anything you would during an in-class lab. You'll just complete the exercises in a different format. These come in two different forms.

One form is the virtual lab. Virtual labs consist primarily of online simulations. Some of them can be quite elaborate, and the technology and realism have improved tremendously. There are virtual chemistry labs that require you to mix precise amounts of chemicals on the screen and manipulate complex equipment as if you were really handling it. Some virtual labs grade you as you complete each activity. Some allow you to redo a procedure if you make an error – others give you one chance only. Some virtual labs enable you to keep notes and answer questions at the end of the exercise.

The second format for online labs is the self-directed lab. Self-directed labs are the exact same labs you'd complete in an on-campus lab, but you perform them on your own in your living room, garage or basement. Along with your textbook and lab manual, you'll be required to purchase a package of lab materials from a third-party vendor or from the college. It should contain all you need to complete every lab during the semester.

Be advised that a package of lab materials does not come cheap. Some run upwards of $500. The withdrawal rate in this course format is usually lower than in traditional labs because students are stuck with hundreds of dollars in wasted lab materials if they withdraw. There is no selling a used lab package as you would a used textbook.

Be sure to research what you need for self-directed labs, and make that purchase long before the semester begins. It may take some time if the materials are being shipped to your home address. You don't want to be without what you need for the first few weeks of labs. *When the package arrives, check the list of lab materials to make sure it is complete.* It is not uncommon for a vendor to make an error or leave something out because it was out of stock. Delicate items can be damaged in shipping. Notify the vendor immediately if something is missing or damaged.

I have taught an anatomy and physiology course with self-directed labs. I pleaded with my students at the beginning of the semester to make sure they had everything for lab. In spite of how much I stressed this, I still received e-mails throughout the semester from students who didn't have this or that in their lab box. Many students felt that they should not be responsible because the vendor left something out, but it was their responsibility to verify that they had everything they needed.

Use proper care when handling and storing your lab materials. Follow all safety directions, which may remind you to keep certain items away from children, store chemicals under specific conditions, and wear latex gloves when handling. *Dispose of everything properly but, before you do, make sure you don't need items again later in the semester.* I have had students throw away their fetal pigs after the first dissection experiment, not realizing that they are used all semester. They then have to furnish another pig, which takes more time and more money.

When the time comes to complete your self-directed labs, you should have a link to them in your online platform. Clicking on this link opens up all of the information you need, including an overview of the lab lesson, step-by-step instructions, and what to submit when completed. Read the directions carefully every time. It's possible that you may omit just one component of the lab and realize afterwards that it was a large percentage of the lab grade. Some labs take several days to complete. If you wait until the day before the lab is due to begin, you won't be able to complete the required activities.

The lab link may contain a file for you to download that you put your lab answers into. Often you'll just type answers in, but the report may get more elaborate. Some self-directed labs require you to take photos during your work, and you may have to label the photos as well. Some of my labs require students to take photos through a microscope lens and label items on pictures, as well as take action shots of themselves performing physiology experiments.

You'll be happy when you finish up your labs, but your responsibilities don't stop there. Next you will need to upload your file(s). This should be a simple process, but a few students every semester still manage to butcher it. At the beginning of the semester you should receive instructions on how to download, manipulate, and upload your lab files. Do not deviate at all from these directions or you'll have serious difficulties.

Sometimes, students submit a word-processing file in some obscure or nonsensical file format that I can't open. Other times I ask that the students make a "pdf" file and submit that, only to receive an uploaded file in the original format. *Never submit a lab file in a different format than the one you downloaded unless you are specifically asked to do.*

If you are given instructions for changing the file *name* (not the file *type*), do exactly what is asked of you. For example, you may be asked to put your last name or student ID into the file name. Avoid adding extra characters in the file name. If you are asked to name a file "BIO101-XYZ-Lab4-Smith," don't upload a file name such as "BIOCLASS(1)(0)(1)-mylabfile4thisweek-Joey." If you are asked to submit one file, don't submit multiple files for separate exercises.

The last step is to upload the file into the online platform. This will likely be under the same lab link that you've been using. Click on "search computer" or "attach file," then find the file on your computer or other device. Click on your file, being careful not to submit last week's file again, then hit "submit." This is a simple skill you should have by now. Nearly all job applications are online these days, and they require you to upload cover letters, resumés and other important files.

Group assignments.

We are inundated these days with buzzwords such as "team oriented" and "collaborative approach." They are on just about every job announcement in any field. You'd get the impression that nobody ever worked in teams on the job until the last few years. The same goes for college work. Be prepared to see these buzzwords and the teamwork format in the college setting, including in your online classes. Your professor may require you to work with a partner or in a group of four on a project or on weekly exercises. Online platforms have separate, virtual workrooms where you and your group can converse and share ideas.

Every online workgroup, not unlike any in-class work group, has that one person who is always missing in action, either absent from class or absent between the ears. The slacker that always seems to have better things to do. In some situations, everybody in the work group may be asked to grade everybody else. If you get graded low, don't make a fuss and cry foul. It's almost a certainty that they gave you the grade you deserved. Better yet, let that person be somebody else.

Assignments to be completed and uploaded.

We have covered completing and uploading lab files, but there are all other types of assignments you may be asked to complete and upload. These include research papers, math problems, pictures for a photography class, or even poetry if you're in an English class. All of the rules for uploading files still apply. Above all, make sure that you upload your files in the correct place in the online platform. Different platforms have various links within them where assignments can be uploaded. Your professor will specify this, so pay close attention.

Online grade book.

Online learning wasn't commonplace until my Ph.D. coursework. The technology provided many new conveniences, but I was smitten with the simplest of things that online platforms offered – an online grade book. Gone were the grades I scrawled inside the front cover of my notebook for all those years. All online platforms have them now. They list the graded items, your scores on them, and how many points were possible.

I've spent many a late hour grading thousands of test questions by hand. I moved to Scantron at some point, but had to walk to another building where the Scantron machine is located, feed the sheets into the machine, and then hand-enter them into a physical grade book. I can't lie. With online quizzes and tests, it's really nice to have forty or more quizzes or exams automatically graded.

We professors request your patience at times. Many online labs, research papers, problem sets, and portfolio items still need to be graded one by one. Online sections often have more students than in-class sections, so we still have mountains of grading to do in certain circumstances. These grades also have to be hand-entered into the computer.

The advantage of an online grade book is always knowing where you stand with your overall grade. Some online grade books calculate a running grade at any given time and weigh certain grades, if necessary. If not, it's not complex math. Add up all the points you earned and then add up all the points you could have earned. Just divide the two numbers to get your percentage grade. You can multiply by one hundred to make it pretty. If you took calculus in high school, this should be a snap.

4.6 Massive Open Online Courses

A variant of the online theme is the massive open online course, or "MOOC." These courses are open to anyone. Most are offered by private companies, although some MOOCs are offered by colleges and universities. They may be free, or fee-based. As they are open to anyone, the enrollment can be astronomical, even numbering in the thousands of students per course. Not surprisingly, the topics and subjects are usually those that have wide appeal.

It is unlikely that you will take a MOOC if you are a degree-seeking student. Most MOOCs are not approved for traditional college credit, although students may receive a certificate of completion at the end. MOOCs usually require online work, including discussion sessions. You may be put into discussion groups with students from all over the world! A relative from Maryland took a series of MOOCs on Egyptology from a university in Britain. She and some of her fellow online students travelled to Egypt for a tour after their MOOC series was completed. Enrolling in a MOOC may be something you do down the road as a lifelong learner.

4.7 Flipped Courses

One of the more recent course formats on the academic scene is the "flipped" course. Flipped courses possess some elements of just about every format I've discussed. There is online work as well as class work. What sets the flipped concept apart is that class time is reserved only for the professor to answer questions. That is, the students complete all other work online prior to coming to class.

In a flipped course, you may watch video lectures and short video clips over smaller sections of class material. There may be online discussion work and online assignments to complete and upload. It is your responsibility to complete all of the instructional materials and save any questions you have for class time, as class time is limited and should be reserved only for those topics students are struggling with.

The flipped course puts a greater emphasis on student engagement. If students are responsible for completing the main elements of the course on their own, they are more likely to take ownership over their learning. If they take more ownership over their own learning, their level of achievement and grades will be higher.

Flipped courses sound great in theory, but do not always work in practice. Students often comment that they have to "teach themselves." Another common refrain from students in flipped courses is, "I'm more comfortable with a traditional lecture." I've heard colleagues say that they end up lecturing in the flipped classroom anyway because an overwhelming majority of their students grapple unsuccessfully with most of the concepts on their own. And quite frankly, some students lack the initiative to do such a volume of work outside of the traditional classroom.

Advocates of the flipped method maintain that it's just a matter of breaking outdated academic traditions. The idea will take off, they say, once enough students have been exposed to the flipped course. The literature on the subject gives flipped courses mixed reviews. My sense is that, like all new instructional formats, the flipped concept may work well for certain subjects and specific courses but won't be appropriate for all.

Be sure to ask around to see what courses and professors are using the flipped method. Flipped courses may not be highlighted in the course schedule. If you do choose to go that route, or don't have a choice, you will need to be especially disciplined and set aside a certain number of hours each day to complete a large volume of work away from the classroom. *Take notes about any concepts that don't quite sink in as you study, and make a list of specific questions to take to class.*

4.8 Seminar And Special-Topics Courses

A seminar or special-topics course may be small-group discussion, an online course, or a traditional lecture. Topics covered are specific and often change from year to year.

If you are admitted to an honors program or honors college, chances are you will be required to complete a certain number of seminar courses. More of your personal analysis and input will be required, instead of just taking a series of tests and quizzes. There is less structure, but professors still have high expectations. The number of students in seminar courses is usually limited, to allow for every student's active participation.

Special-topics courses are often reserved for upperclassmen, usually seniors, and course titles relate to specific majors. If you are a literature major, you may have a special-topics course about one author, or even just one of that author's works. A math major may have a special-topics course on one very specific aspect of a math discipline.

Chances are you'll take several special-topics courses if you go on to graduate school. These courses are something to look forward to. They are an indication that you've really arrived as a scholar. Not that the rest of your college experience won't be intellectually rigorous, but seminar and special-topics courses are your chance to do some really deep and scholarly thinking. They were my favorite courses to take and are now my favorite to teach.

4.9 Self- And Independent-Study Courses

All of the aforementioned course formats have one thing in common: they all have more than one student enrolled in them, and sometimes hundreds. Self-study or independent study means that the course is yours and yours only. Certain majors require one or more self- or independent-study courses to graduate.

These courses are designed to teach you how to develop a topic, do research about it, and write up the findings on your own. You receive guidance from a professor, but you are expected to plan and carry out the study by yourself. An independent study will require you to do some background work and write a short research proposal. The professor will review the proposal and provide feedback. After your proposal is accepted, you will be off and running. You may be required to check in periodically with the professor regarding your progress. At the end of the term you will turn in your final work, which may be a paper, portfolio, and/or presentation.

4.10 Internships And Externships

Your parents may have drilled it into you that you'll have difficulty finding a good job, much less a career, without a college degree. There is a wealth of data showing that college graduates earn much more over the course of a lifetime than those without a college degree. Be that as it may, one of the dirty little secrets of the college experience is that a degree is no guarantee of a job. The Great Recession only exacerbated the difficulties that young college graduates experience in finding jobs. It did not cause them.

With this in mind, it is absolutely essential that you do everything over the course of your college years to set yourself apart from the hundreds or even thousands in caps and gowns sitting around you at graduation. The best way to do this is to complete one or more internships while you're in college. Businesses would much rather hire a recent college graduate who knows the basics of what the company does from the inside, versus hiring somebody with no hands-on experience in the field. Obviously you'll want an internship related to your major. If you want to go to law school, try to find an internship at a law firm. If you are an engineering major, look for internships at small engineering firms or at large companies that have engineering departments. Government entities also offer internships.

You may get into an academic program that requires you to complete an internship or externship. The college may even arrange it for you. *If that is not the case, seek out internships on your own.* Start looking for a good internship long before you think you might enter into one. If you are seeking a summer internship, start looking as early as the previous fall. Talk to those who have completed an internship that interests you and see what advice they have. *If you are somewhat undecided about where your academic interests lie, you still need to look for an internship and have it on your resumé.* This shows a potential employer that you have initiative.

Many young college students say they won't take an internship unless it's a paid one. This is a huge mistake. It would be nice to earn a healthy paycheck while you're learning the ropes, but many excellent internships pay very little. Some internships are completely voluntary, with no compensation of any kind. While there are some battles going on nationwide about the legalities and ethics of unpaid internships, you can't put a price on the experience you'll gain.

If you land a paid internship, don't expect to become an instant manager. Chances are you'll be doing "bottom-rung-of-the-ladder" work. Don't complain – do whatever is asked of you with a smile. Better yet, do *more* than what is asked of you with a smile. Ask questions, and offer solutions when appropriate. *Never forget that a college degree does not mean that you've paid your dues professionally. A college degree gets you in the door after graduation so you can start paying your dues.*

The distinction between "internship" and "externship" needs some explanation. An internship is typically a longer-term commitment. It may last for a summer or an entire semester. In contrast, an externship is usually of shorter duration. It usually consists of shadowing a professional in a certain field for a week or a month. You'll probably be more of a fly on the wall and won't perform any meaningful work while you're there.

Externships are still quite valuable. You get to see what a professional in your desired field does on a daily basis, what his or her routine is, and whom he or she interacts with. It may confirm your desire to eventually enter that field. On the other hand, you may realize that the field is not what you thought it would be. This is also valuable information. It's better to find out before you finish the degree, and start on a career path that you won't enjoy.

This frequently happens to students who think they want a career in a medical field. Many of my students are convinced that they want to be nurses or physicians' assistants until they see blood, have to change a colostomy bag or, worse, see their first dead patient. Some students realize during an externship that they won't be able to handle the stress or long hours. It's not uncommon for education students to find out during their student teaching that they are not cut out for the classroom.

4.11 Clinicals

Students in the health sciences and some other fields are required to complete a certain number of clinical hours, or "clinicals."

Those students may be required to go to a hospital, clinic, or dental office. They shadow professionals, watch procedures being performed by doctors, dentists, or other health-care workers, and perform on-the-job duties themselves.

There are several important rules and regulations that must be followed for clinicals. A few absences or tardies may get you kicked out of the program altogether. You'll be expected to perform certain duties error-free, just like those employed by your host. You may have to submit to drug tests and background checks before and during your time in clinicals. *Don't forget that you are representing your college and its professors – not just yourself.* There are many instances of a college's clinical students getting banned from returning to a hospital or other health-care facility because previous classes had been unruly, unprofessional, or incompetent.

Chapter 5: Bound With Gold: Textbooks And Other Really Expensive Materials You'll Need For Your Classes

If you think you and your parents had sticker shock when you first started looking into the cost of college tuition, prepare for it again when you purchase textbooks. My first college textbooks were pricey back in the 1980s. These days you'd think the bindings must be encrusted in gold. Some college foundations and private organizations offer scholarships now that cover books exclusively. If you aren't lucky enough to land one of those scholarships, you're stuck. *If a class requires you to have a textbook and/or other materials, you need to buy them.*

It's possible to get off easy here and there when it comes to textbooks. Some paperback texts for common classes can be acquired at a reasonable price. But as you progress, you'll need textbooks that are more specialized, and often multiple books per class. I had a history class that required us to purchase six books!

By the time you graduate, you'll probably have spent enough on books to cover a semester's tuition, not to mention spending more on books in one semester than your parents paid in tuition in one semester. It's not going to be cheap, but you can buy wisely. Here are some tips to lessen the financial bite and make the most of those resources you're paying so much for.

5.1 Investigate How To Buy The Cheapest Textbooks

Campus bookstores are typically the most expensive place to buy books. Still, the campus bookstore is the place where the cost of a *used* book might be competitive. It usually has a limited number of used books. Most of those were purchased back from students.

These sell out first, leaving the new, more expensive copies as the only ones left. The campus bookstore will typically tell you exactly what you need for most classes and will have all of the materials in stock. Many professors put their own "readers" and other class materials in the campus bookstore. You can find this out by asking students who have taken the class, or by e-mailing the professor.

The internet is typically your best source for purchasing cheap textbooks. You'll need the International Standard Book Number (ISBN) and exact book title. Every individual book has an ISBN. It's a thirteen-digit code that distinguishes the book from all other books in the universe. Larger sites like Amazon.com carry textbooks, as do hundreds of other retailers and smaller online bookstores. You may have the option of purchasing a new or used book from those sites. Definitely get the used book if it is appropriate for the course. Some textbooks come with codes that allow you to log on to the publisher's website and access course-related material. These often expire after a certain period of time. If you need the code, you may be able to purchase it separately. Check with the publisher.

Used books can often be purchased from other students who have taken the class. You'll find personal ads for books on message boards around campus, as well as in the campus newspaper. You may be able to rent paper textbooks for the semester you need them. Check online for those options.

5.2 Consider Purchasing E-books

Many textbooks now come in electronic format, called an "e-book." It's exactly the same as the paper text but available for use on your electronic devices. E-books are often cheaper than the paper versions. Just don't forget that you'll need a device with you any time you want to use the book. If your battery dies in class, so does your book.

You may be able to rent the e-book. If you do "purchase" an e-book, it might expire on you and go away after a certain number of semesters. Some vendors allow you to purchase the e-book permanently with the option of updating it as time passes.

5.3 Be Mindful Of The Textbook Edition

All textbooks come out in new editions periodically. How often depends on a number of factors. Most textbooks typically change editions every four or five semesters, but some stay on the same edition for an extended period of time. An education textbook I required for a graduate class I taught had just one edition change in ten years.

An older edition will always be cheaper, but there are some pitfalls. Most publishers will try to keep chapter numbers the same from one edition to the next, but page numbers certainly change. Then again, some edition changes are complete rewrites. You'll be lost with the old edition if your syllabus and professor refer to chapter X or page Y in the new edition. This can be a serious matter if you are assigned questions to answer out of the textbook, but the questions have changed from the old edition. Many textbooks have an "international edition" that is very affordable, but chapter and page numbers are different from the domestic edition. Some science materials come bundled together, such as the textbook with the lab manual. This can create a problem when a student just needs one or the other.

You can often get by with a previous edition of the book if changes to the actual content are minimal from old to new edition. I am flexible in my classes in this regard, especially knowing what textbooks cost. I give my students a one-semester grace period to continue to use the previous edition after I have switched to the new edition. *Just realize that you as the student have ownership over acting on those differences.* It is not your professor's responsibility to tell you what page you're on in the old edition.

5.4 Buy The Textbooks And Materials You Need Long Before The First Day Of Classes And Bring Them To The First Day Of Classes

I refer to the textbook during the first day of class. Those who have not purchased it find themselves scrambling to look over a neighbor's shoulder. You may be given assignments out of the textbook on the first day of class as well. If you wait until the last minute, let alone after classes have started, the bookstore may be sold out.

Although I recommend purchasing books off the internet, they can often take weeks to get to you. I can't tell you how many of my students wade through the first two or three weeks of class without a textbook that hasn't shipped to them yet. One advantage of e-books is that you can get an instant download. Buy your books and other materials as soon as practicable and get familiar with them – the format, layout, and order of presentation – before the first day of class.

5.5 Books Are Expensive In Any Format – Get Your Money's Worth Out Of Them

This might seem like corny advice, but *use the textbooks you've purchased.* Invariably, the good students' textbooks are filled with highlights, sticky notes and scribbling in the margins. They know that the book is an indispensible tool to learn the material. I've seen intact shrink-wrap on some of my students' books well into the semester. Other times I've turned to a page in a student's textbook to show them something near the end of the semester, only to hear the classic crack of the spine that indicates the book hasn't been opened yet.

Textbooks can be intimidating, especially in upper-level classes. Most publishers have made strides in recent years in trying to make their textbooks more user-friendly and readable, but certain concepts can be made only so simple. My advice is to just read a few pages per night. Don't get caught up in the details during your first read-through. It will simplify the material greatly. *Never read an entire chapter in one sitting.* You won't retain a thing. Re-read the material more closely after lecture and you will be able to grasp the concepts more easily.

Many of you will have no choice but to sell your textbooks when you are done with them because you need the money. That is certainly no crime. If you can afford it, think about keeping the books in your major and any other books that you found helpful or interesting. I kept all of the books in my major and have referred to them throughout my professional career. I still have my freshman BIO 101 textbook, first edition, from 1987! Believe it or not, it's still a popular textbook at many universities, but it's up to the tenth edition now. I feel like I am, too.

Chapter 6: Your Parts List And Assembly Manual For The Semester: The Syllabus

Although this book is full of information about recent changes in the college experience, one critical item that has remained constant for decades is the class syllabus. The syllabi I give to my students look strikingly similar to the ones I was given in the 1980s. Some of you may have had syllabi in high school, but those will no doubt differ from college syllabi. Whether you are familiar with a syllabus or not, it's the norm to get one for every college class you take. It is a valuable document that provides all of the relevant information you need to know about the class you are taking. Some colleges let their professors use any format they want, while other colleges have a standard syllabus format and template that all professors must follow.

Some college administrators now refer to students as "customers." Many students, and often their parents, now consider themselves to be customers – consumers of higher education. This drives faculty crazy. There are no expectations for you as a customer when you are at the grocery store, cell phone store or home center. All you have to do is pay, and you're right no matter what. Folks my age grew up with this drilled into our heads during our first jobs: "The customer is always right."

A syllabus describes the expectations you must meet to pass the class. Therefore, I know you or your parents might be shelling out big bucks for my class but, sorry, you are not a customer in the classroom. You may be a customer when you deal with Admissions or the Registrar or the Financial Aid Office, but not in the classroom. We are happy to call you a student, learner, mentee or whatever, but customer is out of the question by virtue of the syllabus and the expectations therein that you and everybody on the roster must meet.

That may seem hardcore – even harsh – but it has to be. The syllabus is essentially a legal document, and it's an implicit agreement that you enter into when you enroll in a class. Without the rules and stated expectations of the syllabus, there would be as many sets of rules as there are students. There can't be different numbers of exams, separate grading scales, and different due dates for each student any more than there can be some batters getting four strikes instead of three or some football teams getting five downs when the rest get four. The entire game would break down and be an unfair and unruly mess. The college classroom is no different.

Students too often dismiss the importance of the syllabus, which can lead to big problems. The syllabus isn't just a bunch of papers that can be buried after the first day of class. Lets explore the common topics in a syllabus, what they mean, and how you should approach them, bearing in mind that all professors' individual syllabi will be a little different.

The first page of a typical syllabus is fairly standard material. You'll see the course title, section number, course description and course prerequisites. Pay close attention to the section number. That is the series of numbers and/or letters after the course identifier that separates your section from all of the other sections of that course that semester. In the example, MATH 101.XYZ, MATH 101 is the course identifier and XYZ is the section number. On large campuses, popular courses such as English 101 may have dozens of sections per semester. Memorize your section number and write it on everything you turn in, so that the professor can more easily organize papers if he or she is teaching multiple sections of the same class.

The syllabus tells you what materials you need for the course, including textbooks, online resources, lab materials, portfolio requirements, and so forth. You will see the days and times you meet. Those should match up with what's on your class schedule. You'll also find contact information for your professor or teaching assistant, such as phone number, e-mail, and office location/office hours.

Of particular note is the section that describes how you will earn your grade. A grading scale and rubrics for graded items are listed. The number and types of exams, quizzes, research papers, and team or individual projects may be outlined. These might be presented in a weekly course schedule that lists the course topics and class activities. *Pay close attention to exam and assignment due dates.* Make a note of them on your smartphone, tablet or laptop calendar.

Some professors will go over the syllabus very quickly and jump right into Chapter 1. That's what I did when I first started teaching, because that was my experience as an undergrad. I soon learned the hard way what a mistake that was. I experienced rampant inappropriate behavior and odd requests during my first semester of teaching, which I had not addressed in my syllabus. So I beefed up my syllabus, spent more time going over it on the first day, and hit Chapter 1 near the end of the class period. That solved many issues I'd worked through during the first semester, but some headaches still persisted. For example, students kept asking for extra credit, so I put a paragraph in my syllabus addressing extra credit. These days I spend the *entire* first period on the syllabus. Chapter 1 is for the second day of classes.

Discussion of inappropriate behavior and "dos and don'ts" now constitutes the bulk of my first day, which has become more of a sermon than anything. Some syllabi may put this under the heading of "Class Respect" or "Class Decorum." A colleague of mine even uses the heading, "What You Will Never Do In My Class... Ever." My generation knew these things inherently – not so much these days. Students often see a page or two of text under this heading and tune it out. Rest assured that your professor is as serious about these expectations as he or she is about how you do on exams.

The class schedule is included in the syllabus, and professors will do their best to stick to it, but you may see an asterisk and disclaimer at the bottom. This is because things out of the professor's control can affect the timeline of the course. I was passing out an exam at the beginning of class when the fire alarms went off. Some idiot had called in a bomb threat. My class had to sit in the grass in 100-degree sun for ninety minutes while the building was cleared. Nobody was allowed to leave campus, and we eventually had to scrap class that day. Needless to say, I had to give the exam the next week, which permanently threw off our schedule. One of my students fussed because she said she had planned to be gone that next week! I hope it wasn't one of my students that called in the bomb threat. My exams aren't *that* hard.

Weather, water leaks, power outages – all of these and more can disrupt class schedules – sometimes real fire. I smelled smoke during a botany lab in my senior year. Nobody else smelled smoke until about fifteen minutes later. The TA opened the lab door, and smoke billowed in from the hallway. We all made for the door. When we reached the lawn, we looked up to see twenty-foot flames on the roof. Those flames were right above our classroom! A roofer had accidentally set the roof on fire. Fire trucks poured tens of thousands of gallons of water onto the roof to extinguish the fire, but because of this, the university's herbarium and all of the wood floors in the building were ruined. Of course, I was the only student who left my belongings in the building! I retrieved them when we resumed class in another building two weeks later, ruined from water and reeking of smoke.

It should now be clear that the syllabus has all of the information you should need about the course. A fellow faculty member texted me a picture of "The Most Interesting Man in the World" from the Dos Equis beer commercials, with the quote, "I don't always ignore your e-mails, but when I do, it's because the answer is on the syllabus." It's a bit sarcastic, but spot on.

Before you pepper the professor or teaching assistant with questions about the course details, *look to see if the answer is on the syllabus first*. Nothing irritates a professor more than getting questions about the course that are clearly answered in the syllabus. That's what the syllabus is for!

If you have questions *about* the syllabus, not questions *that are answered in the syllabus*, by all means ask them before anything becomes an issue. I welcome and encourage questions about the syllabus as I go over it on the first day. Typically your professor will be happy to clarify. *Regardless of how in-depth your professor goes into the syllabus on the first day, read it word for word on your own.* Be sure to put it in the front of your class notebook or folder and refer to it early and often. If your instructor posts it online, print out a hard copy and keep it handy. Don't forget that the syllabus is there for your benefit. It states rules, responsibilities, and expectations that, if followed, will go a long way towards helping you to be successful.

Chapter 7: Knock-Knock: Proper And Professional Communication With Your Professors

If you had to guess what has changed the most in the classroom since I first started as an undergrad in the 1980s, what do you think it would be? Perhaps you might say technology has changed the most, and that makes sense. There was no internet then. Another good guess would be how much our body of overall knowledge has grown in the last three decades. We know so much more now about medicine, agriculture and so on. Even further, it's possible you'd tell me that it must be the international influence that's significantly changed the classroom. If you guessed any one of those things, you'd be wrong!

The one aspect of higher education that has changed the most in the last thirty years is the erosion of proper student behavior. Students say things to me that were unthinkable to say to a professor when I was an undergrad. The problem isn't that so many students are inappropriate and rude. The problem is that so many students *have no idea that they are being inappropriate or rude*. Social norms and unwritten rules regarding mature, professional communication have been greatly relaxed. It's a problem in society as a whole, but it's especially pervasive in higher education.

Sociologists consider me part of Generation X, those born between the mid-1960s and mid-1970s. Our elders thought we represented the decline of Western civilization. So said my ninth-grade algebra teacher, Mr. Kirby. About two months into the school year, we entered his class as usual on Monday morning. It was apparent that something was wrong. Mr. Kirby didn't pick up his chalk and litter up the board like he usually did right off the bat.

He looked solemn, even gloomy. Here is what he said to the class:

"Kids, keep your books shut. There's something very important I need to talk to you about. My colleagues teaching eighth grade math have told me over the last few years to expect the worst, most unprepared students in history. They were right. I didn't think it could get worse than last year's class, but your class is beyond anything I've seen. I can only water it down so much. *I simply can water it down only so much.* I don't quite know what to do, but I fear for the future of this country."

None of us knew what to say. Ironically, "common wisdom" states that my generation was the last to be respectful and knowledgeable at a young age. Generation Xers are independent, resilient and adaptable. Scores of students from my high school graduating class went to excellent colleges and universities and have achieved great things.

Mr. Kirby never knew the "Millennials." The first time I heard the term Millennials, referring to those born loosely between the early 1980s and early 2000s, was from a college administrator in the early 2000s. He warned the faculty that we'd be seeing more classroom problems as Millennials entered college in larger numbers. I have taught classes with mostly Generation Xers and classes with mostly Millenials on the rosters. The differences are striking. One thing is for certain – if you are fresh out of high school and headed to college, your professors will be of older generations. *You will be on their terms.* Don't expect them to adjust to your preferences.

Inappropriate classroom behavior is common from those who are the first in their families to go to college. Many of you may fall into this category. It excites professors to see "first-in-the-family" students in our classes. We get a chance to play a role in changing the trajectory of an entire family tree. However, these students have not had a role model when it comes to the college experience and professional environment.

I also see inappropriate behavior from students who have come from affluent backgrounds and long academic pedigrees. I've had children of physicians, lawyers, and Ph.Ds. disrupt class. I've had students with the maturity of middle-schoolers cause problems the entire semester. As far as entitlement, I've seen it all. With apologies to Mr. Kirby, it's getting worse.

If you are a Millennial, I'm not here to disparage your generation. I'm not here to rant about "kids these days." I'm here to help you avoid the behaviors that will get you labeled as a "typical Millennial." If you're the first in your family to attend college, you need the tools to help you act like a college student. Let's open up the toolbox and take a look, bearing in mind that these rules apply whether or not you are a Millennial.

7.1 It May Sound Elementary, But Learn Your Professors' Names

My students call me "Dr. C" as a term of endearment, but many of my colleagues go by "Dr. K" or "Dr. Z" because so many of their students seem incapable of learning the proper pronunciations of their names. I'd like to think that my last name is simpler than those other instructors' names, but I've been called "Dr. Cambridge" or "Dr. Cummings" or "Dr. Cabbage" many times. Your professors will take this as a sign of serious disrespect. That is the last message you want to send. Don't approach a professor about anything until you have learned his or her name.

Be sure to take note of your professors' proper titles and use those titles when communicating with them. Your instructor my have a

Ph.D. (Doctor of Philosophy) in a particular subject, an Ed.D. (Doctor of Education), or an M.D. (Medical Doctor). Note the one thing those titles have in common – "Doctor." Address them as such. You will have instructors and TAs who have master's or bachelor's degrees. In those cases you should use Mr., Ms., or Mrs., but they should be treated with the same respect as anybody with the title "Dr."

On rare occasion you may have a professor say that he or she prefers to be called by first name. I would still address that professor more formally unless he or she appears to be uncomfortable with it. *The professor/student relationship is a formal one.* Treat it as such – the same as you would with your pastor or your boss at work. Your professor is there to enlighten and teach you, not to be your friend. Whatever you do, don't call a professor "dude" or "man" or anything you call your friends when you're hanging out.

7.2 All Communication With Professors Should Be Treated As Formal

You will have ample opportunity to communicate with your professor before and after class, during office hours, via e-mail, and online. Let's take a look at the proper way to approach these modes of communication.

Some professors get to class thirty minutes early. Most do not, and that includes me. I am fanatical about starting class on time, but I'm typically very busy and don't get to class until about five or ten minutes before it starts. Not a week goes by that a student doesn't hit me with drama just as I'm preparing to get class started. *Your professors care about your welfare and well-being, but do not care about your personal drama.* Don't corner your professor with tales of woe right before class. The other thirty students should not have class delayed because the professor is tangled up in your personal mess. If you must talk to a professor about something important on class day, wait until class is over to do it.

Better yet, it is always best to see a professor during office hours. Office hours are specific blocks of time that a professor is available to students. Don't ask a professor when he or she has office hours. Look them up on the syllabus. It's always best to let the professor know that you plan on coming. I suggest sending an e-mail to the professor well in advance, in which you clearly state why you need to stop by. That way the professor will be available and prepared to talk to you. If you stop by unannounced, your professor may be in a meeting, with another student, or participating in an interview committee, and you've wasted a trip.

Not all professors are required to have office hours. Very few of mine did during my undergrad years. I stopped by a professor's office once to ask a few questions about the material we were covering. I could see immediately that he was preoccupied, but I still politely told him my name and why I was there. He said in an angry tone, "What the &#% do you want?" I apologized profusely for bothering him and walked away. Chances are your professors won't be that brusque. Most of your professors will be happy to help you, but don't forget the pre-meeting e-mail.

Don't assume that your professor knows everything about you and your situation when you arrive for an appointment. Softly knock, state your name and the class you're in, and remind him or her about your appointment. If you're seeing the professor about a specific issue, be fully prepared. I have students stop by my office all the time because they are concerned about their grade, but don't know what it is at the moment.

7.3 Any E-mail Sent To A Professor Should Be Professional,

Polite, Correctly Formatted, Mistake-Free, Unambiguous And To The Point

Any communication that is not face-to-face, where body language, tone, and inflection are not part of the equation, can and will be laced with problems. This is especially the case with e-mail. I distinctly remember the first e-mail I ever received from my wife. We'd been together for several years. I knew her well by then. I knew the language and wording that she used when she spoke, and understood the tones and the volume she was prone to (usually a bit loud!) Yet I had to read that first e-mail from her several times over. She used several words in print that she'd never used verbally. I couldn't tell if she was upset. I struggled to interpret her intent. All of this uncertainty – *and I'm married to her*.

Now imagine what a professor, somebody who may not know you from Adam, might think if you send an e-mail that is not crystal clear. Do not leave anything open to interpretation. Here are some examples of text culled from actual e-mails I've received over the years, and how they might be interpreted:

Student: "You really need to meet with me right away. I have some serious issues with my grade."

As for the first sentence, did the student mean to write that, "It would be great if I could meet with you at your earliest convenience," or is he demanding that I clear my schedule immediately, just for him? In the second sentence, did he mean that, "I'm not doing as well as I would have hoped and could use some advice for improvement," or is he putting me on the defensive about how I graded his paper? Putting a professor on the defensive is not to your advantage!

Student: "What do I need to study for the test? The last test had stuff on it that you didn't cover in class."

The first question is impossible to answer. I can't tell her what's on the exam, and all I'm going to suggest is that she re-read the textbook and go back over notes and online material. She didn't need to e-mail me to get that advice. In the second sentence is she complaining about my exams and insinuating that I have not done my job? Never send a "complaint letter" like you'd send to an airline or clothing company. If it's just a random, petty complaint about a test being too "hard," don't waste your time and the professor's. All you've done is single yourself out as a malcontent. I can understand the reluctance to talk to someone in person when there is a disagreement. It's easy to hide behind the computer screen. I've read things sent to me in e-mails that I know the student would not have said to my face.

Don't send an adversarial e-mail, even if you're really mad and believe your anger is justified. In fact, don't send it *especially* if you're really mad. I have a personal policy of never responding to an e-mail immediately if it's gotten under my skin. I always wait a day to cool off before I respond. Abraham Lincoln said that whenever he received a scathing letter, he immediately wrote a response. Then he'd hold on to his response until the next day, when he'd invariably tear it up. If you doubt me on this one, fine, but don't doubt the Great Emancipator.

Not only should e-mails be clear and dispassionate, they should always be written in formal, mistake-free English. Don't use any slang, text message abbreviations, emoticons or the like. Do not misspell words or use the wrong homonym. Use spell-check if you have to. Always proofread before you hit "send." Here is an actual e-mail I've received.

"Mr Cubbagethis is John from ur class I was wandering if u could tel me what we did in class on Tusday. I was miss taken and thot that we didnt haveclass this week is that tru I was a ball bearing in my unclesfuneral."

I really don't know where to start with this mess. There are eight punctuation errors, eight misspelled words and two text abbreviations. The two malaprops are interesting. Who is "miss taken?" Is that a kidnapped beauty queen? And I think he meant "pallbearer" at the funeral. I have a standard reply whenever I receive an e-mail that is so poorly written. "Please clean this e-mail up so that I can read it, and I'll be happy to discuss your issue." Sadly, I have to respond this way to a significant percentage of the e-mails I receive.

Aside from the sloppiness of the above example, you'll note also that he addresses me by the wrong title, does not specify the class he's in and does not give me his last name and student ID number. It is not uncommon to receive an e-mail from a student who does not give a name at all, just a bunch of text. If it was sent from a personal e-mail, chances are I can't identify the student at all. Do not use your personal e-mail for correspondence with the professor or anybody else associated with the college. *Always use the campus e-mail address that the college assigns you.* Some colleges stipulate that faculty and staff respond only to e-mails sent from students' campus e-mail addresses. Here are some e-mail address gems from over the years.

Ohsosexybabe69@*****.com

drinkingitdown@*****.com

momadontplaydat999@*****.net

Insert your own punch lines.

Let's discuss the elements of a properly formatted e-mail. The first item is the subject line. It tells the reader what topic you are covering in your e-mail. Too often this is left totally blank. If your professor sees your e-mail in the inbox and it doesn't have a subject line, the assumption is that it can't be that important. It's likely going to the bottom of the professor's priority list. It may also be mistaken for spam and won't get opened at all. Be specific when typing the subject line.

Never fail to address the professor or TA appropriately with a simple but pleasant salutation. Use the proper punctuation. Here are some examples:

Hello, Dr. Jones,

Greetings, Ms. Johnson:

Good day, Dr. Smith,

Next comes the body of your e-mail. Students' e-mails are typically too short and cryptic to fully ascertain why they have e-mailed or entirely too long and rambling. If it's too short, I end up having to e-mail back with several questions, which starts off a lengthy, days-long e-mail exchange. Here is an illustration of a well-crafted e-mail:

Hello, Dr. Morton,

I am a student in your BUS 201.X2 class that meets on Mondays and Wednesdays at 9:00 a.m. I am enjoying our class immensely. However, I am struggling with some of the concepts in Chapter 5, in particular Section 5.2, which discusses the tax code. I have read the chapter a few times and reviewed my notes, but some of the information is still not sinking in. I know that you are very busy, but could I possibly stop by your office for some one-on-one help?

The syllabus says that you are in your office on Thursdays from 2:00-4:00 p.m. Would you be available at 3:00 p.m. this coming Thursday? If not, I am more than happy to come at a time that is more convenient for you. Thank you so much.

Sincerely,

Julie Jones (student ID 123XYZ)

The body of this e-mail states the issue in one clear paragraph. If it were shorter, I might assume that she has not exhausted all of the study modes she needed to before asking for help. If it took three paragraphs to tell me the same information, my eyes would have glossed over reading it. Professors loathe pages-long e-mails, as does most everybody. In this example, the student has conveyed respect for the professor's time, and values the opportunity to receive help. The professor will appreciate that the student looked at the syllabus first.

Note the polite ending to the e-mail, including the student ID. You can end the e-mail also with the following:

Warmest regards,

All the best,

Be sure to check often for a response if you e-mail a professor. You may not get one right away, but still check. Too many times I've had students e-mail me with something they claim is pressing. I've responded promptly, only to hear back from the student a week or two later. By then your issue may have been overcome by events. I always ask students for a follow-up e-mail after they talk to me about an issue in the hall or after class. Half the time I never receive it.

I've had students come up to me to voluntarily show me a doctor's note after missing a test. Usually these students will send the reminder e-mail because it's something that affects their grade. I'll respond by cutting them a break and saying something such as, "Please come to the campus testing center to take the exam on Wednesday." Wednesday comes and goes with the student a no-show, and there's no response to my response. A week later I receive an e-mail that says, "I can't come on Wednesdays." The campus testing center requires me to put a start and end date on their cover sheet. I'm not going back to change it because you didn't check your e-mail. There is no "make-up for a make-up." If your professor cuts you a break and you don't keep up your end of the bargain, there is nobody to blame but yourself.

If you don't get an immediate response to an e-mail to a professor, bear in mind that he or she may be out of the office at a conference, out sick, or just extremely busy. A common rule of thumb is that, all things being equal, the professor has forty-eight hours as a reasonable window of response time. This does not include vacation weeks or holidays. Professors are human and take vacations just like you. I have received insistent follow-up e-mails from students who write, "I have not heard back so I'm e-mailing again." You haven't heard back because you e-mailed me on July 2. I'm happy to get back to you after the July 4 holiday is over.

7.4 Your Professors And TAs Are There To Help You And Love Doing So, But Don't Hound Them

One of the most rewarding aspects of college teaching is the opportunity to mentor students. Lecturing, running lab, or facilitating discussion is only the beginning of our interactions with students. At times we are also part social worker, therapist, coach, and career counselor. Each semester a handful of students seek out my advice about life choices and life-success strategies.

Students often stop by my office at the same time each week to chat. These conversations make more of an impact on their lives than the best lectures I give. It is particularly gratifying to receive e-mails and letters from students, years after they have graduated, thanking me for the life lessons. Hearing that they used my advice to help get a job, succeed in the workplace, or just be a better human being always makes a tough day better. We all want to believe that we're making a difference.

Hopefully you will form the same mentor/mentee bonds with some of your professors. That said, be very careful not to overwhelm your professor outside of the classroom. Corresponding professionally with them when you genuinely need help or counsel on a semi-regular basis is fine. Approaching your professor before and after each class, sending daily e-mails, and stopping by their office constantly is not recommended. Nothing is worse in life than the friend or relative with whom "it's always something." The same is true for professors dealing with drama-prone students. We want to make you more confident and independent, not enable overly needy behavior.

A student, "Janice," approached me after being late on the first day, and told me she was late because her allergies were acting up. I told her I hoped that she felt better, but asked her to be on time for the rest of the semester. For months, Janice caught me right before class with stories such as "I can't go into class today, I have the flu," or "I won't be in class today because I need to go to the foot doctor."

Later that semester, I was setting up a lab practical exam. I put a note over the window on the door that said, "Do not disturb, exam set-up." Someone still knocked a minute before exam time. I didn't even have to turn around and look. I knew it was Janice. There she was, staring into window, still knocking. The professor who was with me looked and said, "Is that Janice? Is she in this class? Oh, mercy. I had her last semester. Five bucks says that she's going to tell you she has some bizarre disease today." I didn't want to open the door and shouldn't have, but I still did. "I can't be here for the exam. I think might have shingles," she said. I told her that if she did not take the exam that day, I had to withdraw her for missing too much class time, as per college policy. "Drop me?!" she exclaimed. "No, no... I really don't feel that bad after all." I didn't think so.

Another common aggravation involves students who call and e-mail several times to ask if the professor has finished grading something. *Do not badger a professor or TA by continually asking if he or she has finished grading your exam or essay and what your grade is on it.* Professors may have literally hundreds of ten-page papers or exams to grade at any given time, and it can't be done quickly.

On a few extreme occasions I've had to tell students to back off a bit, that they are making unreasonable demands on me and on my time. If a professor implies or openly says that you are hounding to harassing, you have crossed a serious line. Like most professors, I have an "open door" policy during my office hours. There are limits, however, and a professor should not and cannot devote all of his or her time to you. *Avoid being a high-maintenance student.*

Do not ask for special consideration from a professor. For example, your professor can't give you an extra-credit assignment that is not given to the entire class. I've had students who failed to complete work come to my office and ask me to change their grade after the semester has ended. I'm obligated to grade you on what you *actually did* – not what you *wish you could have done*.

Do not disrupt class with complaints about your coursework. During my first semester teaching at the college level, I had a student raise her hand and complain that a test was "too hard." I asked that we discuss it after class, but she walked out without talking to me. She blurted out the same complaint even louder and more rudely after the next test. I took her aside in the hall after class and told her that in-class complaints were inappropriate. I asked her to make an appointment to see me, but she never did.

She made my life very difficult the rest of the semester with constant complaints about her grades. She was frequently late or absent. Finally I told her that if she complained again I'd be forced to ask her to leave. When it was all over, she barely earned a "D" in the course. Just as I was about to leave for Christmas vacation, there she was at my office door, insisting that she needed to speak with me. Before I could say, "Please leave. I told you no more complaints," *she asked me for a letter of recommendation*! I politely declined.

7.5 Most Professors Do Not Like Receiving Phone Calls

You might logically be tempted to say that it's not an unreasonable request to ask a professor to answer the phone or return a call if you leave a voice mail. Your syllabus will likely have a campus phone number where you can reach the professor. Resist the temptation to call. *Professors tend to hate phone calls.* Often we're just not there to answer them. We spend most of our time away from our offices, such as in the classroom, research lab, and meetings. Many professors take sabbaticals and are away from campus for a semester doing research or writing, and can't check their phone for messages. The last thing we want is to be interrupted by the phone when we are working in our offices.

Voicemail messages from students also come with some inherent challenges. Most student voicemails are, not unlike e-mails, rambling messes or cryptic two-sentence bursts that are missing important information. They are usually badly garbled. Most voicemail messages I receive come from cell-phone calls – often dangerously made in cars – and I can make out only about every other word. It's rare that I can make out all of the digits if a student attempts to leave a phone number. It always seems to be the last digit in the number as well. Some students don't even leave a call back number!

Occasionally a student uses the voice mail system options to mark a call as "urgent," or says in the message that it's an emergency and that I need to call back ASAP. Nothing is urgent and nothing is an emergency in higher education. Some of the "emergencies" I've dealt with were students who waited until the last minute to be advised and were frantically calling for an advisement appointment, and students who wanted to ask me what their grade was right before the final. Students also call incessantly during the first week of classes. Your professors are at their busiest then.

I tell students they can call my office, but I prefer e-mail. Professors can respond to you in a more coherent manner in an e-mail because they are able to prepare a response. It's not that we're being curmudgeons. It's better for you if we can gather the information we need before e-mailing you back. My outgoing phone message states that I prefer e-mail correspondence and gives my e-mail address.

For years students would call and ask to be put on a waiting list for classes that were full. I couldn't do that because, with online registration, any student can enroll in a full class immediately if a space becomes available. My outgoing message stated emphatically that we did not have waiting lists. Like clockwork I would have several voice mails a week from students asking to be put on a waiting list. They tuned out after they heard it go to voice mail until they heard the beep, ignoring my entire outgoing message. *Be sure to listen to your professors' outgoing messages carefully.*

If you call a professor who is in a leadership position, he or she often has too many calls – far more than can possibly be returned. Dozens of calls a week would get funneled to me when I was a department chair, whether or not they should have. With all that I had going on, I just did not have time to return ten calls a day. A few more calls always came in by the time I could return the others. This goes for most non-academic offices on campus as well. Imagine how many calls an admissions and records department at a large university receives in a typical week.

Most adjunct instructors do not have a campus phone. They are available only via e-mail or "virtual office hour" on non-class days. New adjuncts mean well and often ask if they should put their personal phone number on the syllabus. The answer is "<u>absolutely not</u>."

I learned this lesson the hard way during my first semester of teaching, when I put my landline phone number on the syllabus and blithely told students they could reach me there. About two weeks into the semester, the phone rang at 4:00 a.m. The phone and answering machine were on the other side of the bedroom so I didn't get up to answer when the caller did not leave a message. It rang again at 4:20 and 4:45 a.m. When it rang at 5:00 a.m. my wife jumped out of bed and answered it. In a state of semi-sleep I heard my wife say "Hello," and then launch into an obscenity-laden tirade that would make the entire Navy blush. When she slipped back in bed I said, "Wow, who was that?" She answered, "One of your #%@& students!" I sat bolt upright in bed. My eyes must have been as big as pie plates. I was sure the student would be in my boss's office to complain about being cursed at. Thankfully that never happened.

What was this student thinking calling that early? If we don't answer that early we are obviously asleep! What did she want, you ask? She had missed class and called to ask if we had a test that day. Again, a major lesson learned on my part during my rookie semester. I naively gave out my personal phone number. It is almost unheard of for a professor to give out a personal phone number to students.

Never, ever look up a professor's personal number on your own and call them on it. Do not wait for a professor at his or her car or show up at their home, even if you believe you have something very important to talk about. This can constitute harassment and even stalking. You may wind up in jail. It may seem like a fringe occurrence, but you'd be amazed how many students do things like that these days. It probably has something to do with both entitlement and the crumbling of personal barriers due to social media.

A colleague of mine, who was head of an academic program, had a group of students who did not get admitted to the program that year corner her at the gym to ask why they did not get in. Apparently one of the students knew she went to the gym every day at that time and told the others. After a stunt like that they will never get admitted, no matter how many times they apply. They were lucky they didn't get kicked out of the college altogether.

In fairness, most of the current and former students I run into off-campus are polite and make harmless small talk. They get a kick out of seeing me in a different setting. If they have moved on to bigger and better things I always enjoy hearing about it. Strange things have happened, though. In addition to the inappropriate call I received at home, I had a student who waited on my family at a restaurant fuss about her grade before she took our order. A student who worked with my mother-in-law asked if my mother-in-law would get class handouts from me to bring to her at work because she missed class. No, Ma'am.

There is another reason most professors prefer e-mail – it provides a paper trail. Students have claimed that I told them this or that, when the e-mail trail said differently. Professors don't want to get embroiled in a "he said/she said" any more than two arguing neighbors do. It's tragic that we have to play "CYA" – nobody enjoys it – but we have to protect ourselves. I've seen many faculty members in recent years be on the hot seat because of allegations of things said in person that ultimately proved to be false. I'm not saying it will be you involved in such a scenario, but some people will destroy reputations and careers for trivial ends.

Getting back to the phone scenario, I have received countless rude voice mails over the years. Needless to say, those calls went unreturned, and in a few instances I've had to take students aside before the next class period because their voice mails were over the top.

If you *must* call a professor's office at the number he or she has given to the class, or another campus number, such as the financial aid office, it is certainly possible that the phone will get picked up. The more likely scenario is that you will have to leave a message. Leave a cordial, short message that clearly states why you called.

Here is an example of an appropriate message:

Beep: "Hello, Dr. Wheeler. My name is John P. Doe, student ID number XYZ123. I am a freshman here at the college. I hope you are having a great day. It is my understanding that you are the director of the honors program. I am interested in applying for the program. I have read the admissions requirements online and spoken to some students in the program, but I still have a few questions about the application process. I know you must be very busy, but if you could call me back when you have a chance, it would be extremely appreciated. Once again, my name is John P. Doe, student ID number XYZ123 and my phone number is 5-5-5-1-2-1-2. That's 5-5-5-1-2-1-2. I will follow up with an e-mail in case that is more convenient. Thank you so much. Goodbye."

This has all of the elements of a good message, and nothing unnecessary. The student has acknowledged his respect for the recipient's time. He indicated that he has done his homework and is not helpless. The reason for the call is unambiguous. Read your phone number off slowly, twice, so that the recipient can hear it clearly and write it down. Do not fail to write the follow-up e-mail right away.

Your responsibilities do not end here. Watch your phone carefully for a return call and answer it. Your chances of somebody from the college calling you back a second time are slim if you do not answer the first time. Also, this is the perfect time to change your greeting to something professional. Get rid of that message with you rapping, using slang or trying to sound cool in some other way. Be sure to have a proper, personalized outgoing message, as somebody from campus may call you and not know if they have reached the correct person. Don't let your inbox get full, such that somebody can't leave you a voice mail.

You will be dealing with people in a professional setting in college. *It's incumbent upon you to learn how to be professional as well.* This will take time, but it's equally as important a college outcome as earning a solid GPA. We in higher education and industry are becoming concerned by the steady decline in professional behavior and decorum among college graduates. I've had a front-row seat for this decline. Around the year 2000 I toyed with teaching high school. My home state offers a "critical needs" teacher-education program that allows those without an education degree to enter the classroom in areas such as science and math. Those entering the program must take a nationally recognized test in the subject they want to teach. I signed up to take the test on a Saturday morning at a local high school.

I arrived early and sat quietly in the hall outside of the room where the test was scheduled. There was earlier testing in progress that was finishing up. Gradually the hall filled with other people there to take the test. Two things struck me. First, I was the oldest person there. I was in my 30s at the time, and the rest were college seniors majoring in education. Second, I was appalled at how loud they were in the hall.

When the noise became unbearable, a proctor came out of the classroom and asked everybody to keep it down because testing was still going on. As soon as she went back into the classroom and shut the door, it became even louder. She came back out again and scolded everybody for the noise. I just sat there and cringed. Within minutes it was even louder than before. She flew out of the classroom in a rage and told everybody to go out into the parking lot until our test was ready. Who were these people who had to be told three times to show some courtesy and respect – basic professionalism – and still couldn't do it? They were people about to *graduate from college.*

Chapter 8: He Gave Me A "C!" College Grades And What They Mean

We all know a few people who carom through life without any desire to improve at anything, but most of us want to get better at the things we do in life. Those who do want to improve place great emphasis on seeing results when they put in the effort. We have to have some form of measuring stick to see results. There must be a uniform manner in which we measure achievement.

At work, it might be how many sales you made in a year, how large your client base has become, or quite simply how much money you earn. In martial arts you work your way up through the rainbow of belts. In golf it's as simple as how low your score has become.

In academia, we measure achievement by using grades. This was not always the case. Colonial colleges didn't use the system of grades we are familiar with. Grades and their cumulative big brother, grade point average, didn't become the norm until the last century. There has been much talk about doing away with the classic system of grades. Some academics and other reformers posit that grades are outdated – that true achievement and improvement are complex organisms that cannot be fully assessed using a few letters. There may be something to this, but grades remain the measuring stick of achievement that we use in academics. Like them or not, you're stuck with them in college.

The standard system of grades is more or less the same that you grew accustomed to over the course of your K-12 years. "A" is excellent; "B" is above average; "C" is average; "D" is below average – and "F" is failure. Some colleges now use the letter "E" or other designations for "F." When I was a freshman in high school I had an exchange teacher, Frau Schwarz, for German class. Our class kept seeing numbers at the top of our graded papers during the first few weeks of the year. Finally one of my classmates mustered the courage to ask what they meant. Poor Frau Schwarz was never told of our American grading system. In Germany they use a "1" for an "A," a "2" for a "B," and so on. She assumed we used those grades here.

Some colleges and universities still use the "plus and minus" system (e.g., B- or C+). Others do not, and therefore an 80.0% and an 89.9% are both a "B" on a standard ten-point grading scale, for example. I've taught at colleges that used the plus/minus system for some letter grades but not others. It's possible you might encounter some other, unorthodox grading scheme here or there in higher education. Be sure to research the grading system at the college you plan on attending. It may be standard across campus or vary from course to course.

There are some grade designations in college that you likely did not see in high school. These include an incomplete, or "I." A "W" is for a withdrawal and a "WF" is for a withdrawal while failing. Another common grade is "pass" or "fail." You pass with a grade of "D" or better and you fail with less than a "D." Some colleges require a better grade than "D" to pass in a pass/fail situation. Below are some words of wisdom about grades in college.

8.1   Grades Are *Earned*; They Are Not *Given*

There is no sugar-coating it. Over the last twenty years there has been rampant grade inflation in the high schools. I attended a local high school graduation in the late 1990s, and about 15% of the senior class graduated with honors. I attended graduation at the same high school about ten years later, and 40% of the senior class graduated with honors. The same trend has emerged around the country at both high- and low-rated high schools. There are several reasons for this grade inflation, but it is not my intent to address them in this book, nor am I casting aspersions on high school teachers, who face many challenges and work very hard.

Grading scales in college classes may be similar to those you had in high school, but what it takes to earn those grades is different from what it took in high school. In other words, it's going to take more effort and dedication than it did in high school to get the same grades in college.

At the conclusion of my first semester as a college professor, a student called to fuss at me about her grade of "D." She kept saying, "I thought I would get a 'C.'" I reminded her that her percentage grade was a 60.5%, which is barely a "D." There were two exams that she had completely failed. "But I thought I was going to get a 'C,'" she exclaimed. I told her that I felt bad for her, but there was nothing I could do. The student didn't understand that her grades reflected her mastery of the material. I could not just "give" her a "C" when she earned a "D."

A colleague of mine who recently taught high school said to me, "We can't fail anybody in high school these days. You get a 'C' for showing up – sometimes for barely showing up." My student had become conditioned to this process. I can't really blame the high school teachers. They are under heavy pressure from their administrators to graduate their students.

I occasionally overhear a student state that "Professor XYZ *gave* me a 'C' on my paper." Students will sometimes come to me and ask why I "gave them" this or that grade on an exam. *Understand that the grade you receive is the grade you earned.*

Professors are flesh and blood and make errors. Once in a blue moon there may be a legitimate slight with regard to grades. But 99% of the time professors are fair and professional graders. If anything, we can be a bit too generous at times. With one hundred midterm papers to grade, an English professor doesn't have time to mark and take points off for every spelling error, even if he or she has software that helps find them.

I give short-answer and essay questions and don't have the time to mark every instance of bad sentence structure or awkward syntax. I'm happy to go over subjective grades that I've assigned, if students want to know how to improve. "What suggestions do you have for me to improve on these types of questions?" is preferable to, "Why did you give me an eight out of ten on this answer." Never put a professor on the defensive over how and why he or she arrived at a subjective grade. It still happens to me a few times a semester. In response, I say that I'll be happy to re-grade the answer, but I reserve the right to take off points for anything wrong that I missed, or intentionally overlooked, the first time. That usually ends the issue.

If you have a small quibble over a subjective grade that is unlikely to be changed, don't complain just to make yourself feel better. Don't spend the entire day stewing over it. It's like complaining about a speeding ticket. Nobody wants to hear it. Just let it go and move on.

8.2 Don't Confuse *Effort* With *Performance* When It Comes To Being Evaluated

I took a class on the philosophy of higher education when I was earning my Ph.D. It was an enlightening class, and the professor was terrific. We spent an entire three-hour class period discussing the philosophy of grades, including the pros and cons of conventional grading. Several of my classmates proposed new, novel ways of assessment; other classmates took the position that grades should be done away with entirely.

One of the students in the class had been having problems in her research courses. She failed one of them, which is uncommon in graduate school, and had to retake it, which infuriated her. Her contention was that, because she had worked so hard and put in plenty of study hours, she should have passed. In her view, grades should be based on effort alone.

But would it be acceptable to us as parents if our children came down with food poisoning, but the restaurant workers were not held accountable because they worked really, really hard? If a bridge failed and we had a bad wreck, would we let incompetent construction workers off the hook because they said that they tried their best?

I have more than my share of students come to me astounded by the low grades they are earning. Their comments usually are as follows:

"I studied non-stop the last few days and still made a 'D' on the exam. How is that possible?"

"I spend three hours a night studying for this class and I'm barely passing."

"I knew it all when I sat down for the test. Then I went blank."

When I hear these statements, I usually inquire about *how* the student is studying. Almost always it's a matter of quantity of study over quality of study. The student is putting in the time, but the study methods he or she is using are ineffective. The student made flashcards, which can be useful, but went through them randomly with no organization by concept. The student spent long hours re-copying all of the notes, but transcribed them without really studying them.

The *effort* was there during study time, but there was no real *learning*. Never put your emphasis on just prepping for an exam. Instead, *focus on learning, and grades will take care of themselves.* The best students are those who are genuinely interested in the material and take the time to understand it.

8.3 Grades Are Definitely Important, But Don't Obsess Over Them

You've been told since elementary school how important it is to get good grades. You may have been grounded as a kid because of bad grades. On the other hand, you may have been given a fancy car because of good grades. Your high school grades certainly factor into your chances of getting into the college of your choice. Nonetheless, you will survive a mediocre grade here or there.

A childhood friend of mine was always at the top of our class in high school. She had brains in places I don't have places, and was cruising to being valedictorian. I always considered her to be somewhat athletic, although she didn't play sports in high school. Little did she know that gym class would keep her from perfection.

One day the gym teacher asked the class to warm up for volleyball by jumping rope. Some of the students in the class grabbed the longer jump ropes and started to do Double Dutch. The gym teacher had never seen Double Dutch and was amazed at this new, creative form of jump rope. She decided that gym class for a few weeks would be nothing but Double Dutch. My friend tried repeatedly to get the rhythm and steps down, but just couldn't get it right. Several weeks later the grades came out, and there it was –

a "B" in gym class. That "B" was her only "B" in four years of high school, but it lowered her GPA just enough to keep her from being valedictorian. That's right – *she missed out on being valedictorian because she couldn't do Double Dutch.*

This would have crushed most seventeen-year olds, but she had a sense of humor about it. She attended Northwestern, who miraculously overlooked the gym grade, and has had a successful career. At our twentieth high school reunion she still laughed about it. I've always admired her for knowing it was not the end of the world.

Grades in specific courses may weigh heavily in students' chances of admission to professional programs. The admissions processes for these programs often operate on point systems. Students get points for taking certain classes and get more points for earning higher grades in those classes. The more points you earn, the more points you can put on your application, and the higher the likelihood you'll get admitted to a program.

I'm pleased that programs such as nursing are competitive. I want the best and the brightest former students to be the ones that stick me with syringes or administer medicine to my children. But I often hear students obsess over whether or not every grade they earn in the class is a "B," which is the minimum, acceptable grade. The 80% becomes a distraction. Those who are zeroed in on the 80% always end up with a 77 or 78% for the course. Always shoot for better than what is needed. *If your expectations are short of excellence, you'll always meet them.*

If you decide to go to graduate or professional school after you earn your bachelor's degree, your GPA will factor into your chances of getting accepted. This will be the last time that your GPA means anything in life. I've reviewed hundreds of resumés from recent graduates over the years who have applied for staff or faculty positions. Unless he or she stumbled through college with "D"s, I couldn't care less if I know the GPA or not. It's rare to see a resumé from an experienced applicant with a GPA highlighted. I have students who drop classes because they might earn a "C" and fret that it's going to ding their GPA. Taking a class over is much less desirable than a small dent in GPA. I can't remember my undergrad GPA to save my life.

If you take a small-group discussion course, you may not receive periodic grades throughout the semester. You'll receive only one, overall grade at the end of the semester. Students all too often have a difficult time adjusting to this model. Contributions to the discussions in these classes are more important than grades on tests or quizzes. If you complete all assignments and immerse yourself in class discussions, you have nothing to worry about.

I taught a small-group discussion class full of master's students. They had taken an accounting class as the first course in their program, and then took my class the following semester. All they had known was rote quizzing and testing with traditional grades throughout their entire undergraduate education and their first class in graduate school. They received a discussion grade at the end of the semester in my class. The discussions early on in the semester were intellectually stimulating and I could tell that they enjoyed them.

Then the e-mails came in droves. Everybody was unnerved because they didn't have a running grade. They seemed lost without it. During the next class period, I dedicated about fifteen minutes to explaining how grades and grading were different in graduate school. It seemed to sink in, but I realized I had to add that to my first-day sermon in subsequent semesters. It reinforced just how conditioned we have made students to grades, perhaps at the expense of actual learning.

8.4 You And Only You Are In Charge Of Keeping Up With Your Grades

The syllabus tells you how to calculate your grade, and your grades should be posted on your class website. *Don't ask your professor what grade you're earning.* Most professors have dozens, if not hundreds, of students and they do not know your grade. Also, do not ask questions such as:

"Can I still get a 'B' in this class?"

"If I get an 'A' in the final, can I still get a 'C' in the course?"

"What do I need to do to still pass?"

No professor can answer these questions!

8.5 Never Stop Attending Class Unless You Complete The Paperwork To Officially Withdraw

If you attend a small college or a for-profit college, you may actually get a call or e-mail from the professor or the admissions department when you miss a few classes. This, however, is the exception, and it's certainly not going to happen if you are in large classes. Remember, *it's not the professor's responsibility to make sure you attend.*

If you need to withdraw from a course, you must take the initiative and do it yourself. Don't assume that a professor will withdraw you. At most institutions, the students are the only ones who can initiate a drop. Professors can't drop students if they wanted to. If you do decide to drop, fill out the proper paperwork and get the necessary signatures, although you may not need the professor's signature and might be able to drop online. Visit the professor during office hours and ask if dropping is the right move from an academic standpoint. *The onus is on you to know the procedure for dropping, as well as any financial aid ramifications.*

If the professor does withdraw you after you bail without notice, he or she may be required to assign you a "WF," which may stick on your transcript. Don't be surprised to see an "F" on your grade report if you bailed on the course and did nothing about it. That was how it was handled when I was in college. My daughter's godfather walked away from school in mid-semester while he was a sophomore. Years later he re-enrolled at the college, only see a slew of "F"s on his transcript. He had to retake the courses and average in the "F"s with the new grades. He eventually finished, went to law school, and is now a successful lawyer, but he still rues the day he just walked away.

In special circumstances, a professor may grant you an incomplete, or "I." This is a temporary grade for coursework that was not completed by the end of the term. In most cases, you have one semester after the "I" is given to complete the required coursework – sometimes called a grace period – but this might vary from college to college. If you do not complete the coursework in the allotted time, the "I" can revert to an "F."

An "I" may be appropriate if you have been doing well in a course but have a personal issue near the end of the semester that was out of your control. I've had students get in serious car accidents the week before the final, or need emergency surgery as the semester is winding down. I've had students in the military reserves get called up to exercises with a few weeks left in the class. In all of those instances I gave the students an "I." If such a situation arises, notify the professor as soon as is practicable. Have a friend or family member make the contact if you cannot.

Do not approach a professor for an "I" if you stopped coming to class because of some personal drama, such as a breakup or a falling-out with a sorority sister. Don't ask for an "I" if something happens to you around midterm. If you can't return to class in a reasonable amount of time, you are better off withdrawing. An "I" is not given so that you can make up half a semester's work later on.

If you receive an "I" it is up to you to follow up with the professor as soon as you are able. You will only be farther removed from the material, and it won't come back to you easily if you wait until the latter stages of the next semester to complete the unfinished work. I tell students to contact me as early in the next semester as possible, but some students dawdle. They contact me a week before the next semester is over and cry foul if I don't have time to get back to them immediately. If completing your work was not a priority for you over the following semester, it's not a priority for your professor at the end of your grace period.

Don't forget that the work you need to complete amounts to extra work for your professor. Approach your professor at an appropriate time and manner, such as during office hours. Remind him or her who you are, what class you were in, and what happened. Don't ask the professor what you missed. You must look at the syllabus, talk to students who were in class with you, and then discuss with the professor exactly what you need to complete to have the "I" changed to a permanent letter grade. Finish the assignments and return them to your professor as quickly as you can. You may have a full semester to complete the "I," but when you begin the process, the professor can set deadlines for completing assignments. An "incomplete incomplete" is nothing to be proud of.

Chapter 9: Present And Accounted For, Sir: Attendance And Tardies

This is the chapter that can be summarized in one sentence: attend every class period and don't be late. That's not exactly Nobel Prize-type advice. Surely your high school guidance counselor or parents beat me to that brilliant tip. I wish it was that simple, but it's more widespread than when I was in school. It's one of the worst things you can do to put yourself at an instant disadvantage, so I want to dig deeper into the subject for your benefit.

9.1 Attendance

While I reference my generation and my college days frequently in this book, I promise that the following anecdote will be my only foray into "when I was your age I had to walk uphill five miles in the snow to school" territory. I earned my bachelor's and master's degrees back-to-back right after high school. Everybody told me to go straight to the Ph.D. after the master's degree. "It will be infinitely more difficult going back to get it later in life. Do it now while you are young and unattached," they all said. I found out later just how accurate this advice was.

In 2005 I decided to go back to school and earn my Ph.D. By that time I was working full time in a position of leadership, operated a microbusiness, was married, and had a mortgage to pay. Furthermore, I had to drive over an hour each way to take my classes. It was brutal, and it became even more complicated along the way when we started a family and my wife had a cancer scare. Through it all – the entire five-year process – I had only one absence.

I tell my students that story in hopes of cutting down on absenteeism and excuses. I also frame the story by highlighting that I'm not rich. We didn't have a nanny to watch my daughter when I was busy with school or a chauffeur to drive me to classes. There was no movie called "Driving Dr. C." My point to the students is that if I can be that dedicated to my studies, I expect the same from them. I know they hate hearing that story, especially if they are taking me for a second course and have heard it before, but I know they think twice before they don't show for class. I'm incredibly proud of that attendance record and want my students to experience that sense of pride knowing that they made it to class even on days when they wanted to be anywhere else.

For years I taught a distance graduate course that required students to attend face-to-face Saturday sessions at the beginning and end of the semester. The students were usually quite dedicated. I was taken aback the first few times I taught the course because students kept e-mailing me to say they couldn't attend the sessions. Their excuses were vague at best. I was talking to a friend about this situation and he asked me one simple question: "Do you teach this course during the fall semester?" To which I replied, "Yes, it's offered only during the fall." He shook his head and looked at me like I was an idiot. "Well, Einstein," he said, shaking his head. "You are aware that the fall is football season?" Eventually I wised up and scheduled the Saturday sessions when the university football team had away games or bye weeks. Attendance went through the roof. Maybe I need to bow to the football gods, but I've showed up to teach many times over the years when my beloved St. Louis Cardinals were on TV in the postseason.

There are countless reasons why you need to be on time and in your seat for every class session. The professor makes important announcements when class begins. He or she may also go over what the class is doing that day, important information if it's a lab and you're doing complex exercises. If you take a class that meets only once per week and you're absent, you've effectively missed a week of school. If you miss one class during a short semester, such as a "Maymester" or summer session, it's tantamount to missing two weeks of class.

Many colleges have campus-wide attendance policies that require the professor to drop you from the class if you miss more than a certain number of classes. One college I taught at had a 20% policy. If you missed more than 20% of the total semester class time, you were withdrawn. *That was far too lenient.* I always ask the students if they would keep a job if they missed 20% of their work – not likely. If so, I want that job!

Attendance is part of your grade in some college classes. In other classes, you might work in groups each day and have a group score at the end of the period. Missing class in those instances will cost you where it hurts – your grade at the end of the semester. In some classes, attendance might never be taken. Regardless, your grade depends on attendance. It's much harder to master the material if you are not in class.

9.2 Tardies

I tell tardy students that I won't entertain any questions that were addressed at the beginning of class. If for whatever reason you do walk in late for a class, *quietly take the first available seat.* Do not walk in front of the professor while he or she is talking. That's happened to me so many times that I had to make a note of it on the syllabus. I was shocked the first time I watched a tardy student saunter across the entire classroom, pass in front of me, block the projector, and sit down as if he was in his own living room.

If being tardy one day is inevitable, don't toss your book bag loudly onto the floor and don't toss your textbook or laptop down on your desk. Be quiet and don't disturb your fellow students. Don't turn to a classmate and say, "Uh, where are we?" Students think that showing up late is not a big deal. *Being late is a big deal.*

I had professors who would lock the door when class started or would openly chastise you in front of the entire class for being tardy, but this is an exception. A colleague of mine won't let students into her microbiology lab after it begins because students work with open flame and pathogenic organisms. Being distracted by tardy classmates is a safety issue.

One of the most amazing professors I ever had was a history professor from whom I took a class on World War II in Europe. He was the most dynamic lecturer you could imagine. He was so compelling that the back rows were full of retirees who routinely audited his classes. I didn't want to be late because I hung on his every word. One day I lost track of time and made it to the classroom late, only to find three other tardy students sitting in the hall taking notes. They, like me, were too scared to walk into his class late. I shrugged my shoulders, sat down and joined them.

Semester-in and semester-out, it always seems that the same few students are responsible for 90% of the tardies and absences, and always seem to be late for the one thing you should never be late for – *exams*. Don't be that student. Any professor will tell you that the looks from your fellow students will be withering if you walk in late for an exam. Your classmates will resent you for disrupting their concentration, and your professor will consider you disrespectful.

Many professors won't let tardy students take an exam after the first person to finish has left the classroom. He or she can't take the chance that somebody who left told you what was on the exam. Most exams are timed, and if you show up late you will have to scramble to finish before time is up. Always leave home early to get to class with time to spare on test day, and be sure to have more materials (e.g., sharpened pencils) than you think you'll need. Don't be the student who not only shows up late to a final exam, but also shows up late for the final exam without anything to write with.

9.3 Other Considerations Regarding Attendance And Timeliness

Never approach a professor after an absence and ask, "What did I miss?" or "Did I miss anything important?" It is not a professor's responsibility to re-create a class for one student who neglected to show up. You are also signaling that you don't think the entire course is important.

Students often approach me and say, "Dr. Cubbage, I'm going to be gone during week four of the semester. My family planned a vacation and everything has been paid for." It's the same story every time – the family's fault. I wouldn't want my child to miss a week of class if I'm paying for it. Did your family not know you were in school? Could you not have taken a vacation when there are no classes? These are sacrifices you must make while you are in school. I've had students drive three hours from the beach, take an exam, and drive three hours back. They sacrificed. Without exception, they were always the "A" students. Plan vacation around school when you are in college – *not the other way around*.

It is important to acknowledge that circumstances beyond our control can happen from time to time. Sometimes we come down with a serious illness, get injured severely or, worst of all, have a death in the family. In those cases, don't be afraid to approach the professor for make-up work. It's not our intent to be ogres, and most professors are usually willing to take such situations into account and work with you to get caught up.

I was pulling onto campus about ten minutes before one of my classes started and saw an accident at the campus entrance. The police were there and it did not appear that anybody was injured, but one of my students had been rear-ended. Of course 1 let her take the exam a few days later. I've also accommodated those in uniform whose jobs caused them to miss a class here or there.

Before you approach a professor under these types of circumstances, please read the policies on make-up work in the syllabus. Just saying, "I was sick and need to make up the test" won't cut it. Most importantly, don't lie about why you were absent. Professors have heard it all.

Professors' watches or clocks are the timepieces of record when it comes to the moment class should begin. I require an out-of-class assignment to be turned in before class begins in a particular course I teach. A few times per semester, a tardy student wants to argue with me by claiming that he or she was on time according to his or her watch. That argument is a non-starter.

Even though my attendance was excellent in grad school, I had the occasional tardy and absence as an undergrad. That being said, *I never made it my professor's headache.* The last thing I would have done was draw attention to myself after I'd been irresponsible. If you are absent, get with a classmate about what you missed, although the rest of the class may not want to help you. If you were late, you disrespected them as well. Given that possibility, *just don't be late or absent.*

Chapter 10: Don't Be A Fool, Follow The Rules: Proper Classroom Behavior

I loved coming to class in my college days. I enjoyed completing classes and racking up credit hours. My combined transcripts show about 240 total credit hours. While some of those credit hours were preparatory hours for my master's thesis and Ph.D. dissertation, and a few were for online classes, most of them were for traditional, in-class coursework. That's a staggering amount of time in class – I estimate about 2,000 hours total.

In all of that time, I can recall only one incidence of rude or inappropriate classroom behavior that a professor had to address. I took an engineering course pass/fail as an undergrad, and two guys behind me would talk on occasion. One day their voices carried a bit too far. The professor turned around, caught their eyes, and walked towards them. You could feel his anger as he pointed at them and scolded them loudly, ending with, "…and if I have to tell you again, you'll both be packing up your apartments and driving home to become roofers. *Have I made myself clear?*" Believe me, they didn't make a peep the rest of the semester.

It occurred to me at that moment that it was the first time I'd seen anything like it in nearly four years of college. I saw professors chew out students for poor work and slack performance, and there were a few times an entire class had to be told to pipe down when group discussions became a bit lively. But over the course of nearly four years I'd never experienced a professor need to address disruptive, "high school-ish" behavior.

We viewed our professors as keepers of wisdom and knowledge that we were seeking. We never thought of ourselves as customers. It was the professors' world – we were just interlopers in it. They were accomplished, intelligent people whom we wanted to emulate, even if they were occasionally crotchety, curt or arrogant with us. They were not teachers of the thirteenth grade. *They were college professors.*

Times have changed. Halfway through this current semester I've already dealt with a dozen instances of rude and inappropriate behavior, including:

- Dozens of instances of texting in class.
- A tardy student walking in front of me while I was addressing the class, even though I told the students on the first day of class to never do it.
- Two students giggling and passing notes when we were watching a video.
- Four students arriving late for an exam and one of them bringing nothing to write with.

That brings me to the worst offense of the semester. One of my classes has a quiz at the beginning of each class period. I collected the completed quizzes and was going over the quiz with the class, when a student walked in late. He walked right up to me while I was addressing the class, and interrupted me in mid-sentence.

Student: "Can I still take the quiz?"

Dr. C: "Let's talk about this after class."

Student: "But if I hear the quiz answers, then I can't take it later."

Dr. C: "Sit down, please. I think it's best if we talk about this after class."

Student: "But…"

Dr. C: "I am addressing the entire class right now, which you've disrupted. One more word and I'll have to ask you leave. *Please sit down.*"

He looked at me, puzzled, and took a seat. I could see the body language of some others in the class. They were wondering, "What in the world is this guy thinking?" After class he approached me again.

Student: "Can I still take the quiz?"

Dr. C: "The quiz is not the issue here. Do you realize that you disrupted the entire class because of your own personal issue, and all of that after you walked in late?"

Student: "But if I heard the answers, then how could I take the quiz?"

Dr. C: "You are missing my point. Would you walk in late for church and interrupt the pastor in mid-sermon?"

Student: "But I really need these points."

Dr. C: "Please read the portion of the syllabus that covers tardies and absences. I went over this on the first day."

Student: "I missed the first day."

Dr. C: "Read the syllabus."

Student (looking at me like I'm the jerk): "Well, are you going to let me take the…"

Dr. C: "It's clear that I'm incapable of making my point with you. If I can't reason with somebody, the conversation is over. I'm sorry, but this conversation is over."

I use this incident to reinforce an important point. No matter what I said to this student, he didn't realize that walking up to me in the middle of class was the real issue. Equally troubling was the fact that *he had no idea that his behavior was inappropriate*. While this type of situation is rare, it is happening with more frequency. It should *never* happen. Let's take a look at dos and don'ts when it comes to classroom attitude, conduct and behavior.

10.1 Be On Time And Accounted For In Class, Every Class Period

Being late signals to the professor that you can't manage your time. It also telegraphs that you don't respect his or her time, not to mention the disruption you cause when you're late. Even if you slink in late into the back of a large lecture hall, you've been seen by your professor and by the students you've disrupted.

Being absent indicates that you had better things to do. If you are physically able and aren't going to give the rest of the class Ebola, you need to shoot for 100% attendance. The professor knows that the more absences a student accrues, the more difficulties he or she will have with that student. Given the steep cost of college these days, every day you miss class is money squandered. It's like making payments on a car you never drive. You are missing out on knowledge and wisdom that, unlike a car, you can use for life. If you are receiving grants or scholarships, you are cheating taxpayers or the scholarship granter if you don't attend. If your parents are paying your tuition, think of what they'd say if they knew you missed class because you slept in or went to the lake.

10.2 Don't Wait Until The Last Minute To Ask Questions – Timing Really Is Everything

I have given literally hundreds of lab practical exams. I tell students to be ready to go as soon as I open the door on lab practical exam day, and I reiterate that online in the days leading up to the exams. This rarely works as planned. A few students are usually in the lounge at the end of the hall when I open the door, their books still strewn across the lounge table. I am finished with the instructions about the exam by the time they've packed their book bags and wandered down the hall to the classroom. Once in the classroom, several students end up lingering by their bags while they turn off their phones, ask other students if they can borrow a Scantron sheet, or dig in their bags for a pencil. Inevitably a student asks if there is a pencil sharpener in the room.

All of these things should have been taken care of before the exam began. *If you are required to be at a certain place at a specific time, do not be in the bathroom, down the hall or anywhere else. Have at least two of everything that is required, and be ready to go.*

Some questions from students are more palatable than others. Sometimes the timing of student questions is completely unpalatable. A few years ago I was passing out the first exam of the semester in one of my classes. After I had passed out half the exams, a student blurted out, "Are you going to take off for spelling?" My response was, "If I say 'yes' or 'no,' are you going to spell any better or worse at this point?" This question is a no-no at any point in time, but it is unacceptable to ask that question or any other *as I'm passing out an exam.*

10.3 Class Time Is Not The Time To Present Your Personal Issues Or Grievances To Your Professor

Keep personal drama to yourself. Don't blind-side your professor with personal issues right before class, and save anything of a sensitive nature for your professor's office hours. Even more importantly, don't bring up your personal issues *during class. Don't raise your hand and ask a question or make a statement that pertains to you only.* The rest of the class does not want to hear it, and your professor is in no position to address it.

I often have students ask why I took points off of their papers as I'm going over the exam. My answer is always, "Please see me after class." I grade hundreds of those questions in a typical week. I have no clue at that moment how and why I scored every one of them a certain way. Am I supposed to stop class and re-read your exam right now? Discuss your exam after class or visit the professor during office hours.

Another thing to never say to a professor during class is, "Your tests are too hard." If you say this, then it's a safe assumption that you're not doing well in the class. You've just told the entire class that you can't handle the material. *You don't want to draw attention to that fact.* You also questioned the professor's competence and professionalism in front of the class – not a good idea.

10.4 Do Not Use Technology To Communicate With Anybody During Class

This is another situation where behavior is stratified by age. My students over forty never have their smart phones out; my students between twenty-five and forty will get them out from time to time but try to hide them; my students under twenty-five just whip their phones out anytime during class, with no regard for the rules.

Not only are you telling your professor that what is on your phone is more interesting, and more important, than the class material, you are distracting those around you. Often I see students finish a quiz, put the quiz aside and get their phones out until I pick the quizzes up. Students around them are still taking the quiz, and this distracts them.

I subbed for a colleague one week while she was having a baby. I noticed all of the students had their phones out, and I had to ask repeatedly to put them away. When the professor returned, I asked her if she lets her students have their phones out during class. She responded that it had become so rampant that she had just given up on policing it. Most professors have not, and will not, throw in the towel in this regard. In the early days of cell phones it was actually a bit funny when a phone with a cute ring tone went off in class. It's not funny anymore.

Pay close attention to the rules on the syllabus regarding in-class use of technology. Professors may dock your grade if you use your phone during class. A college roommate of mine was kicked out of the class for reading a newspaper in the back row. He wasn't kicked out of class for a day – he was kicked out of the class for good. It took a trip to the professor's office and much groveling for him to be let back in.

Rules about using technology can get tricky when it comes to laptops and tablets. I strongly encourage my students to take advantage of technology when it comes to their studies, and my classroom in particular. My stance is that you can use these electronics for note-taking, picture taking during lab, or research in class, as appropriate, but no personal communication is allowed.

A colleague of mine says this to any student caught with a phone out or surfing the web: "All of us have the goal in life of being happy. If you'd rather be somewhere else, by all means go be somewhere else. We'll both be happier."

10.5 Do Not Waste Your Time Or The Professor's By Asking

For Special Favors

Your syllabus should be clear about your grade and what is expected of you for the semester. Don't ask a professor to deviate from it because you are struggling. Here are some common favors and special breaks you should not ask of your professors.

"Can we have some extra credit?"

You have plenty of assignments to complete to earn *credit* in the classes you take. Focus on that. You'd be surprised how little an extra-credit assignment changes an overall grade. It generally helps only if you are right on the borderline. A typical extra-credit assignment is not going to lift you a half or full letter grade – not even close. It's really a false god.

In the interest of full disclosure, I offer my classes an extra-credit opportunity each semester. My students can donate blood for some extra credit. If they are not comfortable doing that or cannot donate due to health reasons, they can bring a donation of cat or dog food for a few bonus points. When the semester is over I fill up my truck with the donations and take them to the local animal shelter. It might move the needle for a few students, but it's not going to make up for a semester of poor work.

Keep in mind that the professor can't offer one student what he or she doesn't offer the entire class. Don't ask to write an additional paper or do an extra assignment to earn more points. College is an audition for the working world. The working world does not offer extra credit.

"Are you going to give us a study guide for the exam?"

Everything that's been covered in class is fair game on an exam, as is material in the book that the professor did not have time to get to. We want to teach you how to prioritize and organize information on your own. A study guide defeats this lesson. I don't recall ever getting a study guide as a student.

I once passed out a study guide to one of my classes, which was actually a study guide that another professor had put together for the course. It was a classic case of, "No good deed goes unpunished." Some students said the study guide was too long; some said it was too short. Some students fussed that material was on the study guide but not the exam; some fussed that material was on the exam but not the study guide. I have never passed out a study guide again after that.

You already have a very expensive study guide. *It's called your textbook. Read it.* Most textbooks have summaries at the end of each chapter that serve as excellent study guides. If I were to give my students a study guide, I'd just photocopy those pages and pass them out. A professor may pass out study guides or rubrics, but let the professor give them to you if he or she chooses. *Don't ask for them.* It makes you appear helpless.

"Is this going to be on the test?"

Of all the questions that sound worse than fingernails on a blackboard, this might be the one. When you ask this question, the professor interprets it as you asking, "What is the minimum I have to do?" It's a dead giveaway that you are a slacker. It sends the message that you have no interest in learning the material, just passing the test. *Study as if everything will be on the test.*

"Can we have more time on the exam?"

I generally give my students ample time to finish in-class or online quizzes and exams, but they are definitely timed. A basketball player can't ask the referee for five more seconds after the buzzer has gone off. Life is timed. Your job duties down the road will be timed. I tell my pre-nursing students that, if they get into a nursing program, their clinical work is timed. They won't get thirty minutes to take somebody's blood pressure. *Use your time in college to practice working under pressure, including time constraints.* You'll be glad you did.

"Will you drop a quiz?" "Will you drop our lowest exam grade?" "Can we retake the quiz to get a better grade?"

Read the syllabus. If accommodations are not there, don't ask for them. Your professor is under absolutely no obligation to give them to you. A professor might have five sections of the same class in a given semester. Out of fairness, the professor can't change the rules in one section and not change them in all sections. Changing the rules for all sections is a huge hassle and creates a grading nightmare.

"If I am on the borderline, will you round my grade up?"

This question inevitably surfaces during the last week of class. This is one of the many situations where your behavior and attitude throughout the semester will work for or against you. If you have been lazy, problematic or chronically late, don't expect to be rounded up. You haven't earned that benevolence. It's possible that your professor has gone easy on the class throughout the semester, such as dropping a lowest quiz or, yes, giving some extra credit, *so you've really already been rounded up.*

Don't make the mistake of thinking you are on the borderline when you really aren't. I often have students say, "I'm only two points from a 'B.' Why won't you round me up?" In reality, you are *two percentage points* from a "B," which is twenty (or more) actual points away from a "B." That is, your overall percentage grade is a 78% and a "B" requires a minimum of 80%. In these instances a student was often absent for a twenty-point quiz at some point during the semester. That was the twenty points the student needed to earn the higher grade.

Chapter 11: The Complaint Department Is Five Hundred Miles Down The Road: Solving Campus Grievances The Right Way

Most of the professors whose classes I took as an undergrad probably never received a single complaint. Students never complained to their faces and never dared to go over their heads to the Department Chair, Dean or administration. These days, even the best professors rarely go through a semester without hearing complaints.

This is due to many factors, including societal shifts away from inherent respect for authority, the "student as customer" mentality, and high school administrators and teachers who'd rather cave than spend the time and energy fighting a bogus complaint from an angry parent. I hear it from high school teachers all the time.

College faculty lament the softer stance that college administrators often take on bad behavior, and they themselves perhaps aren't as strict as they once were. But baseless, small, silly complaints aren't going to go anywhere the way they may have in high school. Faculty don't have to answer to trivial complaints at all.

I need to make a very important distinction. This section is dedicated to addressing complaints about academic and minor classroom-related issues. *It is not intended to discuss the complaint process or steps to be taken when there are more serious allegations at hand.* These include unwanted sexual advances or sexual harassment, quid pro quo (e.g., sexual or other favors for grades), physical altercations, and any other allegations of a criminal, unethical or truly negligent nature. If you as a student believe that an incident or persistent behavior that rises to this level has occurred, *you need to contact the proper authority immediately*. This could be local police, campus police or student services, depending on the situation.

Below are some scenarios that might give rise to a complaint that does not fall into the more serious category, and what to do in those situations.

11.1 If Your Complaint Is About Something Minor That Cannot Be Fixed, Let It Go

What do I mean when I say that you shouldn't complain about something that "essentially cannot be fixed"? When I was the leader of a large academic department, students would often come to me to complain about their professors. Here are some examples:

- "His tests are too hard."
- "I don't like his teaching style."
- "She expects us to know too much."
- "He isn't friendly at all."
- "I don't like her accent."

In those instances, I would say, "I'm sorry you feel that way, but what would you have me do about it?" Then I usually get a blank stare. I'm not being flippant when I ask that question. In all seriousness, what could I possibly do? Am I supposed to fire her because she is challenging you intellectually and making you work? Am I supposed to write him up because he has a foreign accent? There are no remedies in these situations, and all you do is single yourself out as a malcontent when you complain about them.

You'll find that most professors don't hold a grudge and are consummate professionals when they interact with students, but coming to them with insignificant complaints only runs the risk of alienating them. This is especially the case if you make it personal. Therein lies a life lesson that you can take beyond college. *Never needlessly alienate anybody whom you're going to rely on later or who has power over you.*

A classic example involves a student who told me that she was getting ready to file a lawsuit against an entire nursing department at another college. She claimed that she was the victim of reverse discrimination because she did not get accepted into their program. Discrimination is unacceptable, and sometimes legal action is a necessary recourse, but it became evident that she had absolutely no proof to back up her allegations. In fact, her statement was, "I don't have any real proof, but I *know* that it happened."

She intimated that maybe there had been no discrimination, but the department would get scared, want this behind them, and let her in. The first thing I told her was that I was not a lawyer, and I did not want to dispense any advice that could be remotely construed as legal advice. Nevertheless, I pointed out that if she won her lawsuit, she ran the risk of making life difficult for herself. "How is that possible?" she exclaimed. "If I win the lawsuit, they'll have to accept me into the program."

She had not considered that the faculty in that nursing program would be accused of unethical, if not criminal, behavior if she filed the lawsuit. Their reputations would be in question and their careers could hang in the balance. They would have to take time out of their busy schedules to gather paperwork, give depositions, and possibly appear in court. If she won her lawsuit, *these same faculty members would be her instructors for the next two years, and those years would probably be unpleasant.* This had not occurred to her.

Steer clear of fellow students who always whine about the professor or want you to join them in a frivolous complaint. These students have problems with every professor in every class they take. They never succeed, and their attitudes are toxic. *If you hear them complaining, walk the other way.*

11.2 Don't Make The Professor The Bad Guy By Making You And The Entire Class Stick To The Rules

The rules in the syllabus are there for a reason. They create a level playing field and fairness to all students in the class. They set not only academic but behavioral expectations that are designed to build responsibility and accountability.

Nowhere are rules in my syllabi as explicit and clear than about make-up work. My syllabus states that there is no make-up work for any reason, but I make exceptions if a student has a verifiable illness or death in the family. I discuss this in detail on the first day, and leave nothing open to interpretation. However, every semester I still get approached for make-up work by students who have lame excuses or no excuses at all.

If you are allowed to make up work for any reason, thank the professor profusely. He or she is being inconvenienced by helping you, even if you don't realize it. Whatever make-up work you complete has to be given to you separately, graded separately, recorded separately and given back to you separately. This takes time, and it is not part of our normal routine or workload.

Complete the make-up work without questioning it. If it means anything to you, you'll move heaven and earth to get it done as per the professor's conditions. Say, "Thank you so much, Dr. Jones. This is more than fair, and I appreciate your mercy. I'll have this completed immediately." Then follow up.

Do *not* say any of the following:

Professor: "I'll give you a break just this one time. Please come to the Testing Center to take the exam on Tuesday."

Student: "I can't take the exam Tuesday. I have a softball tournament."

Professor: "As a make-up, please complete the review questions at the end of Chapters 2 and 3. This is due by the end of the day tomorrow."

Student: "You'll need to give me more time. I'm going to the beach tomorrow."

Professor: "You've been a good student thus far, so I'll cut you a break. You can still turn the paper in, but out of fairness to your classmates it cannot be for full possible credit. The most you can earn is fifty points out of one hundred."

Student: "That's not fair. Since I was late by ten minutes you should only take ten points off."

Professor: "This is not the flea market or the Persian bazaar. There is no haggling. If you don't like the break I'm giving you, you're welcome to not take it at all."

Those are actual exchanges I've had with students who asked for make-up work.

If you don't complete the make-up work, accept the zero that you will surely receive. *Don't ever ask for a make-up for a make-up.* If it wasn't a priority for you to be in class to take an exam, it's not a priority for your professor to deal with it.

11.3 If You Feel That You Have A Minor Classroom Issue

That Needs To Be Addressed, Always Talk To The Professor First

I want to reiterate that I am not referring to rare but serious issues such a sexual harassment or some sort of physical altercation involving a professor. Clearly you would not see the professor first in those situations, and should seek out the proper authority immediately.

Approximately 90% of the complaints I've received from students taught by professors I supervised involved grades. Actually it's closer to 100%. It usually took a bit of peeling back the layers to get to that fact. Common things I heard were statements to the effect of, "He gave me a 78% on my essay when I deserved at least a 90%" or "She promised she would give us all five bonus points but then said she wasn't going to." In these instances the policy was that the student should speak to the professor first, but it was really common sense to do so.

We professors can be absent minded (shocking, I know). Grade disputes are often due to a simple misunderstanding. Don't be intimidated about talking to your professor. Be respectful, and never put the professor on the defensive right off the bat. If you are hostile or confrontational, the professor will be less willing to listen to you.

There are several situations the professor will want to be informed about. At the top of the list is cheating. Professors are proficient at noticing instances of cheating and taking the appropriate action, but cheating does slip under our radar sometimes. If you know it's taking place, we want to know. Don't say anything to the person cheating. Turn the matter over to the professor, and don't think of yourself as a snitch. If one of your classmates is cheating on an exam, quiz or research paper, *they are cheating you*. Also inform your professor about class rules that are being broken or situations where classmates' behavior is interfering with your safety or making you uncomfortable.

11.4 If You Bring A Complaint Directly To Your Professor, It Is Not Advisable That You Take Your Parents With You

Parents, I know you'll have your hackles up over this one. You may be spending big dollars to send your child to college. It's fantastic that you've spent the last eighteen years planning for your child's college education. If you've been financially and emotionally invested in seeing your child earn a college degree, chances are your child will be equally as dedicated. Good job, Mom and Dad.

Professors respect what parents do to ensure their children's success, but simply stated, *they do not want to see students' parents in their offices*. This is for two reasons. First, before you toss this book into the fire pit because of that sentiment, this situation is a *legal* one. As per the Family Educational Rights and Privacy Act (FERPA), once your child has enrolled in college, his or her educational records are private and confidential. *If a professor speaks to you about your child's grades, academic progress, attendance record or anything else of the like without the child's written consent, he or she would be in violation of federal law.*

The refrain is always the same when a professor informs a parent of this legal situation: "But I am paying for this!" Be that as it may, the student is enrolled, not the parent. Who is coming up with the cash is irrelevant to the college. It's not the same as marching up to the high school when you think your kid has been slighted. So if you are a helicopter parent, you'll need to accept that there is no helipad on a college campus.

Federal law doesn't exactly make for stimulating reading, but visit the U.S. Department of Education's FERPA website (familypolicy.ed.gov), and research this law in detail. The institution has the obligation to inform the student of FERPA rights. The student can waive his or her right to academic privacy and confidentiality and consent to the disclosure of educational records by going through the proper channels with the college and signing the appropriate paperwork. The consent must be signed and dated, specify what records apply, state the purpose of the disclosure, and identify the party or class of parties to whom the disclosure may be made (34 CFR § 99.30).

Second, if you come to campus, call our offices, or e-mail us about your child's business, you are not letting the child learn how to handle his or her affairs. Part of what we are trying to do – above and beyond just relaying course material – is act as life mentors to make independent, self-reliant young adults (and they *are* adults). They can't grow if you keep attempting to solve their problems. You may have good intentions, but you're hurting more than helping if you interject yourself into their college affairs.

I still, however, always agree to speak to parents when they request to see me and the student has waived FERPA rights. The student usually sits there motionless and silent, deeply embarrassed, as Mom or Dad runs roughshod over the conversation. And that's the problem. Most of the time, parents do not come to talk to a professor about how the child is progressing or what the child can do to improve – it's to lodge a complaint about the child's grades.

Mom or Dad sits down in my office under the impression that the child should have a "B" because the student told them he or she has earned "B"s on everything. The situation changes quickly when I show the parents that all of the student's grades thus far in semester are "D"s and "F"s. And you should see the looks on the parents' faces when I tell them that their kid has a bunch of absences and tardies that he or she neglected to mention. In the end, the parents almost always leave the meeting furious with their child, and they apologize for wasting my time.

11.5   There May Be An Occasion When You Have A Potentially Legitimate Grievance That Cannot Be Resolved With The Professor

Professors are humans, just like anybody else. We have bad days. We say things we wish we could take back. There can be a rare lapse of professionalism that negatively affects the class or an individual student. If you feel you have a bona fide grievance that needs to be addressed, and it could not be resolved with the professor, you have the right to take the issue farther for redress.

In those instances, follow the college's grievance policies and procedures to the letter. They are almost always in the college's student handbook, and can be found at the student services or student ombudsmen's offices. They list the steps you must follow. This will almost always involve seeing the professor first. Next will likely be the professor's department chair, then the dean, and so on. Some colleges require you to see somebody in student services after you've talked to the professor. It's up to you to confirm the proper path that has been established for resolving your issue.

With a consumer-based mentality and a culture of instant gratification these days, students often jump up several levels in the chain of command, thinking that they have a better chance of resolving the situation in their favor. I've seen students go directly to the college president, usually via letter or e-mail, about grades or not getting accepted into an academic program. The college president will just send the issue back down the chain to the appropriate level. All you've done is waste your time, and the president's. You also imply that you think you are too special to follow the rules.

Students will also "pinball" between student services and anybody in the academic chain of command who happens to be in his or her office. All you'll do is confuse yourself and those who want to help. Things have a tendency to get off message, and the details of your situation can evolve in ways that won't best serve you. If you've ever played the game where ten people stand in line and relay a message down the row from person to person, you know how a message can get mangled.

Have all the facts and relevant documentation, such as all of your quizzes, research papers and exams, when you show for an appointment with the appropriate person. Have all written correspondence with the professor with you. Don't leave anything out because it does not support your case. If you conveniently omit the e-mail that doesn't work in your favor, it will come to light eventually.

Don't try to speak for the entire class. Don't say, "The entire class is failing." The person you are seeing can only deal with you and your issues. If others from the class want to come forward, they will have to do so of their own volition.

The professor is innocent until proven guilty, just as you would want to be if the roles were reversed. The burden of proof is on you. If you are complaining about your grade, *it is your responsibility to prove that an error has been made*. A he said/she said situation will only muddy things, even if you are in the right. Nobody can make a professor change a grade without a good reason. If you earned a 75% on a research paper, the administration or professor's supervisor can't re-grade it and give you an 80%. You may have the right to have your grades reviewed for errors, but you cannot get a grade changed just because you didn't like it.

11.6 There May Be Situations When You Should Absolutely Bring an Issue Forward

Hopefully, if not probably, you will go every semester, even your entire time in college, without experiencing anything that should be brought to the attention of the professor's supervisor. Be that as it may, *the impression I don't want to give is that, if your professor is doing something that is truly unprofessional, you should shut up and live with it – not at all.*

Once again, I am not referring to the situations such as harassment, intimidation and so forth. Those situations should be referred to the proper authority without hesitation. There are other situations in which students may feel reluctant to come forward, but it's the right thing to do. Here are some examples.

The professor is chronically late or consistently misses class without any explanation or communication.

If we professors expect you to be on time every time, we should do the same. You can expect to find your professor on time and prepared for class every day, but occasionally a situation might arise with a tardy professor.

One evening, late in the semester, I was walking through the hall where my department's labs typically meet, on my way to the Scantron machine. It was around 6:30 p.m., and there were several students sitting in the hall. Our evening classes always begin at 6:00 p.m. I asked the students if they were on a break, and I was told, "Dr. XYZ is late again. He's been this late every time." I asked the others if this was the case, and they indicated that it indeed was. Later I asked the instructor for his side of the story. It ended up being a simple misunderstanding that we remedied immediately, but I wish the students had come forward at some point earlier in the semester. I could have resolved the situation sooner.

The professor is not following the syllabus or is violating campus or departmental policies.

You may believe that something in the syllabus has been changed or ignored that is negatively affecting you or the class, or that the professor is in violation of written policy. You have the right to come forward if you believe that this cannot be worked out with the professor.

For example, the grading scale should never change. If the syllabus says that you need a minimum of an 80% to earn a "B" in the course, then a "B" should not require an 85% at the end of the semester. Your grades are confidential. If the professor has a habit of letting students see each other's grades, such as putting graded quizzes in a pile for students to pick up each week, the professor's supervisor needs to know.

As outlined in Chapter 6, the professor may have a disclaimer in the syllabus that states that he or she has the right to make changes based on extenuating circumstances. The professor has every right to do this, and most of the time, changes are for the students' benefit.

The professor is not covering the material on the syllabus, or is using class time to discuss topics unrelated to the course.

Professors are almost always on task and on message in class. Class topics will follow the specific list and order presented in the syllabus.

Allowances should be made for occasional discussions about events or issues unrelated to the class that don't negatively affect the class, any individual student, or the grand scheme of the course, nor do they eat up significant portions of class time. I taught a class on the evening of 9/11. You can bet that we talked about it as a class for several minutes that night. If the professor and class talk for a few minutes about the big game or a cool vacation the professor just took, it will actually help you establish rapport.

Many courses cover a wider variety of subjects than students expect. This is a good thing. We want you to think in interdisciplinary ways. We want you to connect scholarly dots that you may not have known even existed.

But there are still limits. Your computer professor shouldn't go on about politics all period long. Your chemistry professor shouldn't take up an entire class period talking about his golf game.

You can prove that your grade is incorrect, and you could not resolve the situation with your professor.

The vast majority of students who come to me to complain are there to complain about grades. Students often misunderstand the grading scale or are hoping for a miraculous grade change, but can't quantitatively prove that they have earned a higher grade.

Sometimes I've put a "1" in a grade column online when I meant to enter a "10." Most professors are not math professors, and even smart people make mistakes. All it takes is a quick e-mail or discussion after class, and your professor will be happy to look into it.

If the professor offers no resolution and you can prove your case, don't be afraid to come forward. Please remember, though, that the onus is on you to prove that the error exists. The bank isn't going to credit you fifty bucks if you can't prove that it made a mistake. Similarly, don't go to a professor or his or her supervisor without every graded item, or at least a list of all of your grades, which can then be compared to the professor's records.

Chapter 12: Your Turn To Grade: The Student Assessment Of The Professor And Course

Near the end of every semester, or once per year at some institutions, you will get to evaluate your professors and the courses they are teaching. The name of the assessment instrument differs from college to college, such as "course survey" or "instruction evaluation," but the concept is the same. For simplicity it is usually called "Student Evaluation of Teaching," or SET.

Until recently, the professor would pass out written SET forms and leave the room after designating one student to collect them when the class has completed them. The package would be sealed, and either given back to the professor when he or she returned or delivered by the student to a designated office on campus. These days they are almost all given online. Your professor should give you a heads-up about the window of time to log on and take the survey, and you will probably receive an e-mail to your campus address that provides you with instructions for completing it.

Many professors, but certainly not all, view SETs with a tinge of cynicism. Some professors believe it's like having kids rate their parents. You might hear a professor say in private, "Who is some nineteen-year-old college freshman to evaluate me? I'm a Ph.D. with thirty years of teaching and eminent research under my belt."

Put another way, what if baseball batters were able to rate the umpires on how well they call balls and strikes? What if the umpires' jobs depended on getting good ratings from the batters? The strike zone would be as small as a saucer, and the game would be meaningless.

The SET can still be a useful tool that professors use to improve their teaching. The SETs themselves are fairly straightforward, but all too often the students don't fully understand their purpose, and colleges and universities don't do a good enough job of explaining to students how the results are used. Here is an explanation of the major aspects of typical SETs, and how to complete them in a useful, productive and meaningful way.

12.1 Be Sure To Complete The SET Accurately And In Full

The SET is your chance to give your input on the course and the professor, *so by all means take advantage of that opportunity.* Even if you are enrolled in five or six classes, complete every one of them. Don't wait for a second or third reminder. Some colleges won't release your grades until your SETs are completed, but this is becoming rare.

SETs can range from a few to a dozen or more questions about the instructor and the course in general. Often there are two separate sets of questions: one that applies specifically to the individual professor and one that pertains to the course content.

Be careful to keep the SETs straight for each course. Know the rating system on the survey. You should receive detailed instructions at the top of the survey, just like a quiz or exam. Read them carefully. I've had a student come up to me sheepishly and say, "Dr. C., I think I completed the survey for Psych 201 thinking it was yours for BIO 210." Other times I've heard students say, "Can I take the survey again? I think I misunderstood the rating scheme and gave you a bad evaluation when I meant to give you a good one."

12.2 The SET Is Not Intended As A Forum For You To Slam Your Professor Because You're Unhappy With Your Grade

Ask any professor, and he or she will tell you this is the biggest flaw with SETs. One of my responsibilities as a campus leader was to monitor the SET results for all of my instructors and keep track of the overall grades from each section every semester. There was always a strong correlation between the mean class grade and the SET results. Sections with a lower average class grade rated the professor lower and sections with a higher average class grade rated the professor higher.

There is always one student in every class who clicks the lowest possible rating on every question. Some students click the first thing they see to get the SET over with, but normally it's the students who have an axe to grind about grades. If your professor were that incompetent, he or she would not be employed at the college. Nobody is that bad at everything. It's not always easy, but separate your feelings about your grade from your evaluation of the professor. Your professor didn't summarily fail you at everything during the entire semester. Find it in you to return the courtesy.

12.3 Evaluate The Professor Based On His Or Her Abilities, Not On How Happy He Or She Made You Or How Much You Were Entertained In Class

Whether or not you "like" a professor is completely irrelevant when you sit down to complete the SET. If you asked for some sort of special break and did not get it, or you did not do well in the class, you may have convinced yourself that the professor is a jerk. Do not unfairly retaliate by giving the professor a poor evaluation.

One of my most experienced and skilled adjunct professors caught half her class cheating on an exam. The guilty students received zeros, and it dropped them a letter grade in the course. The professor's SETs had been stellar for years – always among the best in the department – but the ratings for this class were in the gutter. Clearly, the majority of the class retaliated on the SET. *The fact that she discovered cheating should have resulted in high marks.* There was a time when those students would have been kicked out of the class permanently, if not the college, so they should have counted their blessings for only getting a zero.

You may not like challenging exams, but great professors give them. They are trying to get the most out of you. They are trying to get you to understand the importance of the course material and the necessity of proper classroom behavior. Professors often joke about being "mean until Halloween." This is a reference to being strict at the outset of the semester to command the students' respect. It's not something that should trigger a bad evaluation. Everybody has a different personality, including professors. That should have no bearing on how you evaluate them unless you believe that it interferes with their job performance. Stern professors are that way for a reason.

Be honest on the SET, but be fair. While you shouldn't give a poor evaluation for trivial reasons, you shouldn't inflate the ratings any more than we should inflate your grades. If there is an area where you truly believe the professor could improve, by all means reflect that in your rating.

One of my professors in graduate school was a tenured, full professor who had been a prolific researcher and head of a large research lab. He brought millions of dollars of grant money into the university over the course of his career. Before he passed out the evaluation he said, "I am a tenured, full professor who is golfing buddies with the movers and shakers at this university. If for some reason you want to use this evaluation to say how much you don't like me, I don't give a #@%$. I'm not losing my job.

But this old dog will still learn new tricks. If you honestly think there is something in the course that I could improve upon, I will take it into consideration."

Of particular note is how adjuncts are affected by their evaluations. Full-time professors have all manner of work-related items they are responsible for throughout the year, such as professional development, committee assignments, course development, grants, research and so forth. Adjuncts are usually in the classroom only, so their SETs carry significant weight in their term-to-term employment.

Make no mistake – if an adjunct is performing poorly you have every right, if not the responsibility, to make the appropriate marks on his or her SET. But before you skewer an adjunct on the evaluation for selfish or petty reasons, just remember that he or she is working extremely hard for modest pay and often nonexistent employee benefits. If adjuncts undeservedly end up in hot water over low evaluations, not only is it unfair, it can affect their livelihood. They may be tempted to go easy on their classes so that they can keep their jobs. That does not help you as a student.

I watched helplessly as a wonderful adjunct was let go due to low student evaluations. She was dedicated to the students and engaged in the classroom, but the students kept complaining that she was "too hard." The only crime she was guilty of was asking her students to achieve. It's difficult to find adjuncts to teach the course she taught, so the students' reward when she was not hired again was the course being offered less often.

Professors will tell you in a weak moment that from time to time we all have that section from "heck." The laws of statistics don't apply to the roster. One would think that we'd have about the same percentage of high achievers, moderates, slackers, and malcontents in every section we teach. If only that were the case. Instead, it always seems that section A of a specific course is full of brilliant, dedicated students, while section B absorbed all of the problem students.

I've observed that the students in the morning sections of certain courses are far superior to the students in the late-afternoon sections. At any rate, adjuncts often teach only one section in a given semester. That section may turn out to be full of students with bad attitudes who decide to gang up on the professor in the evaluation. The professor has only that one SET to be judged on, and an injustice has been done.

12.4 Make Use Of The SET Comment Section

Most professors, including adjuncts, are open to objective suggestions for improvement. You can add such comments in the comment section. Unfortunately most students just breeze through the SET and don't leave any comments. I can't tell you how many times students have praised my teaching in class but didn't comment on it on the SET. I encourage you to make comments on any SET, be the comments positive, negative or both. You can even think them through before you begin the evaluation. Just be sure to put the proper thought into your comments.

If you really enjoyed the professor and his or her skills in the classroom, you can expand on this in the comments. Be sure to be specific. That way the professor knows what is working and will continue to do those things. For example, you might say, "I enjoyed his 3-D image projection in class. It was an excellent learning tool."

Confine your comments to the professor's job. Some of the comments I've had on my SETs over the years include, "He wears cool shirts" and "He has pretty blue eyes." I'm flattered, and those comments make my day, but they don't add anything useful.

The most glaring and avoidable mistake students make on the SET is writing off-message, personal, scathing or profane comments. Again, you have every right to make negative comments if the professor and the college need to hear them, but negative comments should be specific. Don't write a rambling, two-page diatribe. If things were really that bad, you should have approached the professor or his or her supervisor earlier in the semester or, quite frankly, you should have withdrawn.

Negative comments should be objective, no matter how upset about something you might be. Write them professionally. Your comments will be disregarded out of hand if you curse or name-call. Don't exaggerate or make up critical comments to justify in your mind why you earned a bad grade. I received these two comments on the *same SET* one semester:

"This dude was crazy. He was the worst professor I've ever had. I'm thinking about transferring so I don't have to have him again."

"Dr. C is amazing. His class transformed my life. He's the best professor I've ever had. I was going to transfer to another college, but I'm staying here so I can take him for more classes."

The second quote is a bit of grade inflation on the student's part. That kind of praise is nice but I know I'm not *that* good. As for the negative comment, it's personal. I've been a "Faculty Member of the Year." I've had glowing student evaluations and classroom observations from my bosses. I refuse to believe I was the worst professor any student ever had, even on my roughest of days. That comment went nowhere, but if the student had been more specific, it's certainly possible that something productive could have come out of it.

Here is an example of a negative comment I received that was fair and useful:

"He really didn't seem to be into the material. I had heard that he's an enthusiastic professor, but that was not what I experienced. He seemed to plod along in his lectures. He told anecdotes as if he's told them a thousand times. Some of his presentation materials were outdated and referenced a previous edition of the textbook."

My first reaction was irritation – the comment seemed arbitrary. Maybe the rest of the class thought I was enthusiastic, and enthusiasm is such a subjective construct. But I took a deep breath and tried to understand why the student wrote that comment. As it turns out, I had taught multiple sections of that particular class every semester for years. I taught that class exclusively in some semesters, including back-to-back sections. There were times when I didn't really look forward to that class. I realized that I was burned out on it. I decided to teach fewer sections of the course, and began rotating it in and out of my schedule. Now I look forward to teaching it.

Chapter 13: I'm Taking My Talents Elsewhere: Transferring Credits To Another College

Our elders often spent their entire working lives with one company. My father spent his entire career with the telephone company. Even as recently as a decade ago, most Japanese companies promised new employees lifetime employment. This practice is all but extinct. You may change jobs, if not career paths, more than a dozen times in your life.

The same trend has emerged in college attendance. Transferring from one college to another was certainly possible decades ago, but it was uncommon. It's probable that older college graduates you know spent all four years of college at the same institution. They never had a reason to transfer to another college, or take classes at another institution and transfer them to the primary institution. And most of our forebears never took another college class for the rest of their lives after graduation. Also factor in that there weren't as many colleges and universities fifty years ago as there are today.

We move around much more than our grandparents did. New knowledge and job skills are needed throughout one's life these days. More education is needed to get promotions and stay current. We have access to online learning now as well. Lifelong learning has become paramount. Therefore, you may attend several colleges at different points in your life. I started out at a small, private liberal arts college, took a class at a community college during a summer, and transferred after my sophomore year to a large state university.

Changing colleges may give you new opportunities, but it also creates serious administrative and academic problems. Some credits are non-transferable. Others transfer within a state-college system, but not necessarily outside of that system. Some transfer as electives only. In certain instances, credits are transferrable but are considered too "old" and must be retaken. College XYZ may be on the semester system, while other colleges nearby are on quarters or trimesters. The American college system is a true hodgepodge in this regard. Here are some suggestions for a smooth transfer process.

13.1 Get Familiar With How To Submit Transcripts

Transferring from one college to another, or going back to college after many years away, will require you to submit all of your existing transcripts – *all of them* – to the college you want to attend. Remember that one class you took at ABC College twenty years ago that you almost forgot about? You'll need to get that transcript.

Until recently, the only option was to have transcripts mailed. A transcript was considered official only if it was sent directly from one college to another, without you handling it at all. If you picked that transcript up at admissions and records and opened the envelope yourself, it was no longer official.

Today, just about every college or university can send them electronically either via their own transcript system or through a third-party service. They still have to be sent directly to the receiving institution. You can't have them sent to you and then forward them. Transcripts cost money, and costs vary from college to college. Some will send one copy for free and charge you for any others, but most will require payment for any copy requested. Contact the college you want to attend and ask them for the specific location, e-mail address, and point of contact to have your transcripts sent to. You'll need that information when filling out the transcript request form. The last thing you want is your transcript being sent to a college maintenance or security office. I've seen that happen.

13.2 If You Plan On Transferring To Another College, It Is Your Responsibility To Make Sure You Know Exactly What That College Requires From You Academically

Look up the requirements for your major at the institution you want to transfer to. You may have taken a 100-level math course but they require a 200-level course. Tailor your electives towards those that the college will accept, and also tailor them to fulfill your requirements before you actually transfer. If you're going to study computers, for example, it makes no sense to not take computer-oriented electives.

13.3 If You Plan On Taking Summer Courses At Another Institution, Make Sure Your Home Institution Will Accept Them

I strongly advocate for taking summer classes, but don't start down this road unless you are sure that they will transfer. I made this mistake myself. It was my understanding that I needed a computer course as part of my program of study. I took a computer course at a community college to satisfy this requirement when I was home one summer. I went to transfer it but the college would not accept it. As it turned out, I needed a general computer course but had taken a programming course. They were not the same. After much begging, the college accepted it as an elective, but I still had to take the general computer course.

13.4 Courses May Have The Same Or Similar Titles, But The Content And Credit Hours May Be Different

Many colleges offer courses in the same subject for majors and non-majors. The majors' course in chemistry might be CHEM101 and the non-majors' course might be CHEM100. The non-majors' course will not be as rigorous, and the college you're transferring to may not accept the non-majors' course. The same goes for courses in the same general subject that are taught in two different departments. You might take a course about trees in a landscape-architecture course, but the destination college may not accept it because it does not have a biology (e.g., BIO) prefix.

The number of credit hours for a course can vary between colleges and universities. You may have a 3-credit interpersonal-communications course on your transcript, but the transfer institution requires a 4-credit course. Courses on the quarter system can be particularly tricky. I don't suggest enrolling in them if you plan on transferring at some point, because quarter credits rarely equal semester credits.

13.5 Science Courses Without Labs Are Not Equivalent To Those With Labs

A community college I worked at had high rates of course transfer both in and out, which is not uncommon. Most of the time, the admissions department would evaluate transcripts to determine what would transfer in, but many times I was asked to do a "course evaluation" if there was any doubt whether or not a biology course was equivalent to those we offered. I was usually lenient, and if the course was loosely equivalent to what we offered, I recommended that the college accept it in transfer. I hated to see a student take a similar course over again, especially if he or she had earned a good grade.

The one scenario in which I could never accept a biology course as an equivalent was when the course did not have a lab and ours did.

On several occasions students stated, "You require microbiology. I've taken microbiology at another college." Yet the microbiology course they took elsewhere did not have a lab component. The lecture material may have been completely identical, but without a lab, it's not the same course.

13.6 If You Have Been Out Of College For Several Years, Be Prepared To Retake Some Classes

Not all colleges and universities are equally accommodating when it comes to accepting transfer credits, especially when it comes to how long it's been since you took the course(s). After years in environmental consulting, I decided that I wanted to get into education full time. I had been teaching part-time at a local community college – my heart was set on higher education – but I briefly decided to look into teaching high school biology.

I investigated getting a degree in secondary education at a local university. When I talked to the department chair she said that they would not accept my introductory biology credits because they were "too old." At that point they were all of twelve years old. It's not as if they were from the 1930s, and I had earned a master's in zoology about seven years prior. She was adamant that I retake BIO 101 and 102. Even after I told her that I was currently *teaching* those courses at the college level, *she still insisted that I retake them*! I politely ended the conversation and moved on.

13.7 Overseas Transcripts Can Be Particularly Difficult To Evaluate

Sending transcripts back and forth overseas will become more common as the college experience becomes more international. There are a few service companies that evaluate overseas courses and determine U.S. equivalents. If you or someone you know has to go through this process, allow plenty of time, as it can take months to get the process completed.

Chapter 14: The Great Campus Shopping Mall: Utilizing Campus Services

Walk into any shopping mall in America and the first thing you'll see is the mall's map kiosk. It is dominated by what makes the mall money – the stores – with an occasional maintenance room, bathroom and administrative office here or there. Now imagine what you'd think if you walked into the mall only to see the map littered with enough maintenance rooms and administrative offices to rival the number of stores.

Higher education has undergone this transformation in many respects. Until the last ten or fifteen years you'd see mostly classroom and laboratory buildings on just about any campus map. Sprinkled here or there would be dorms and athletic facilities. After a bit of perusing, you'd finally find the couple of buildings on the map that housed all of the non-academic, administrative departments.

Take a glance at any campus map these days and you'll see the non-academic square footage on campus on par with the academic square footage. For starters, it seems as if the athletic directors are the new college presidents. New athletic facilities are strewn across nearly every campus. Similar sports that once shared a field not only have new, ultra-modern fields of their own, they have new, ultra-modern *practice* fields of their own. Mushrooming athletics also need coaches, assistant coaches, assistant coaches to the assistant coaches, graduate students, trainers, psychologists, and on and on. Of course, these folks need facilities of their own. If you throw in the multiple recreation centers that all students have access to, not just the student-athletes, most large universities could probably host an Olympics these days.

The newest, fanciest buildings that don't have a direct tie-in to academics will likely have "development" in the title. This is the most recent name for fundraising. Granted, the army of non-academics inside may be working hard to secure funding that might help your academic department, but you'll ask yourself why your history class isn't in a building that nice.

Whereas admissions and records, the registrar, and counseling may have been housed in one building for decades, many campuses now have gleaming new buildings for each of them. Even if they have been shoehorned into existing buildings, most institutions have created scores of new administration and service positions, such as diversity and inclusion staff, counselors, financial aid officers, and accreditation officers.

There has been much debate in academic circles as to whether this all takes away from the reason you're there – to get an education – or whether all of these new facilities and their services enhance the college experience. I won't open that debate in this book. What is important is that you become familiar with this new side of the modern college experience and know how to utilize these services to your advantage. After all, *you're paying for them*! For better or for worse, the sharp increase in college tuition in recent decades is at least in part due to the construction, operations, maintenance, and labor costs associated with non-academic college growth. Below are some helpful tips to get your money's worth from these services.

14.1 Get Familiar With Campus Services And Where They Are Located

Many non-academic facilities were likely pointed out to you during the campus tour. A friend of mine recently went on a campus tour with his college-bound daughter. Their guide took them to eight non-academic buildings and all of one classroom building over the course of the tour.

On large campuses, the formal tour cannot possibly cover every street and every building. You should take a self-guided tour to see all of the nooks and crannies on campus. Small campuses may still have most student services in one or two buildings, but walk the halls to get familiar with it all. In some instances the only land available to develop for a new services building was way across campus and, now, two buildings with related services may be far flung from each other.

A common mistake that students make is assuming that everybody who works on campus can answer every question. I have students make advisement appointments with me, only to have them ask questions about financial aid that I can't answer. Financial aid offices say that some students make appointments with them and ask questions about academics that they should be asking their advisors. Students come up to me after class and ask what the deadlines are for applying to various academic programs. I have no idea. Knowing who to ask what will save you many squandered hours bouncing around campus.

14.2 Investigate Exactly How Different Services Are Rendered

Campus service offices are like hair salons: some take walk-in traffic and others require an appointment. If you need to use a campus service and wait until the last minute thinking you'll be served immediately, you might need an appointment and miss a deadline. Campus services are like any other businesses. They are extremely busy or slow depending on the time of year, day of the week, and hour of the day. Naturally, just about any campus office is going to be slammed during the first few weeks before and after the first day of classes. I've taught on commuter campuses and heard students rage in the parking lot because they drove an hour to campus but could not get their business taken care of – no matter that it's the day before classes begin.

Be prepared to deal with service-related headaches. This is not an indictment of campus support staff. A college is a complex organism with many moving parts. Sometimes things get lost or misfiled. Sometimes policies and requirements change, even entire computer systems, and it takes time for employees to adjust. Just as not all professors are top-notch, some administrators can be mediocre or difficult to deal with.

I came up one credit short of the requirements on my program of study in graduate school. My advisor told me that she and I could design a one-credit independent study, which had to be approved by the department chair via a specific form. I made an appointment with the department chair and drove an hour to his office, only to have him no-show. Thankfully another faculty member agreed to sign in his stead, so I took the form to the registrar's office for final approval.

After waiting in line for forty-five minutes, I received the paperwork to take to the bursar for payment. It rang up as over $1200, when it should have been about $400. The bursar said, "That's what it costs for a 3-credit independent study." I reminded her that it was only a one-credit course, but she would not approve it. She sent me back to the registrar.

After another thirty minutes waiting in line, the registrar told me that the college had done away with one-credit independent studies. I would be on the hook for another $800. I pulled up the course catalog on her computer and showed her the verbiage that specifically said an independent study could be one to three credit hours. "We haven't changed that online yet," she replied.

Knowing I needed her help, I sweetly asked her if she could just do this simple favor for me. She refused. "Look," I said incredulously but still trying to keep my cool, "I'm pointing right at *your* website, which says right here that this is a legitimate option, and it's been approved by my department. What harm is there in you signing this?" She sneered and refused again. I was forced to walk away.

One visit to the Dean of the graduate school later that day solved everything. He saw me immediately, said I had "catalog rights" and made the change on the spot, saving me $800. But I still spent an entire afternoon on a wild goose chase that was not of my making. I could and should have complained, but I let it go. If you have a similar ordeal, just make sure you persist and go through the proper channels. Try to stay patient, don't put anybody on the defensive, and things will eventually work out. These situations should still be rare. Support services on campus are generally happy to serve you.

14.3 Take Care Of All Health Insurance Details Before You Need Health Care In College

I needed to see a doctor for something minor during my freshman year in college. I went to the health office only to discover that the small campus didn't keep a doctor on duty – only a nurse who could dispense limited services. I made an appointment with an off-campus doctor. When that visit was over I found myself calling my father on the office's phone because I didn't have any health-insurance information with me. I had never discussed with my parents what I needed to do if I became sick or injured while away at school.

This is an area that has become much more complicated since those days. Love it, hate it or know nothing about it, Obamacare has changed the health insurance landscape. If you are a high school graduate about to attend college, be sure to talk to your parents about what health insurance you have, what it covers, and what it costs. Take a copy of your health insurance card to school with you.

Ask how health care is handled on the campus where you plan on attending. Medium- and large-sized universities have dedicated student health facilities. You may be paying for them as part of your fees. I took a racquetball off the eye at the recreation center during my senior year and had to be taken via ambulance to the student health center because I lost vision. That health center was the size of a small hospital. I waited almost two hours to be seen, during which time I gradually regained sight in the eye that was hit. They never asked for payment after I was seen. Be sure to research where your student health center is located, what services it provides, and what if any payment you'll be responsible for.

If you are on medications, be sure to have a list of them that can be given to a health-care professional who might need to know them. Include the dosages and any other relevant information in your list. I know it can be personal, but you might want to mention any health issues you have to your roommate or residence assistant so that they are in the loop.

Here is one last piece of unvarnished advice in this area. My buddy's mother was a campus nurse at a large university for decades. She said about one in three students who came in were seeking treatment for sexually transmitted diseases. *Do not let that be you*!

14.4 Take Advantage Of All Available Campus Recreational Opportunities

You will never again have all of the recreational options available in one general location than you have in college. Most campus recreation centers are better equipped and more diverse than just about any private gym.

During graduate school I had a long-term relationship come to an end. I searched for some way to channel the negative energy of the heartbreak and decided to get back in shape at the campus rec center. The first day I walked into the center, I was overwhelmed with how much it offered. There were multiple weight rooms, a world-class natatorium (pool), basketball courts, racquetball courts, a climbing wall, and just about anything else you can imagine. By that point I'd been in graduate school for a year and couldn't believe I'd gone that long without using those resources. I had been paying for them.

I ended up losing thirty pounds and buffing up. The rec center offered free fitness evaluations as well. I signed up for one after about nine months of intense training and scored in the top 3% in fitness on campus. Those days are certainly over – I could probably score in the top 3% at pizza consumption now – but I look back fondly over how much I utilized that rec center.

14.5 Use Campus Resources Not Only To Look After Your Body, But To Also Maintain Proper Mental Health

For all of the excitement and joy of the college experience, it can still affect us in negative ways. Homesickness is not uncommon. The stress of grades and a challenging major are omnipresent. We can find ourselves in all manner of complicated social and relationship problems.

When I was an undergrad, there was a person or two on campus who were available to listen and help if we students were having psychological troubles. None of them were professional counselors or mental health professionals. Just about every college campus has a dedicated, professional counseling group these days. *Don't hesitate to make use of them.*

Many campuses have "life coaches" available for students who are having some doubt about where they're headed in life or for those simply looking for some inspiration. Life coaches can help you with motivation and staying on the right track academically.

Also available are officers who deal exclusively with students with disabilities via the "Americans With Disabilities Act" or "ADA." If this applies to you, make contact with them during the application and admissions processes. The application may ask if you have a disability and the school may extend its outreach. They will work with you to complete the proper documentation that you can take to your professors to work out "reasonable accommodations" for your disability in the classroom.

I have never had any issues accommodating students with disabilities, and I am always happy to help. You'll find that your professors will gladly work with you and your situation. It is a two-way street, though. We professors ask that you be consistent with the accommodations after we have reached an agreement about them. I ask my students with disabilities to notify me twenty-four hours in advance of any episodic instance when they need accommodations, such during an upcoming test, so that I can get things arranged. All too often I never get the reminder from the students. Some semesters I've taken quizzes or tests to a testing center for a disabled student, only to have him or her show up at the classroom because, "I felt like taking the quiz in the classroom today instead."

14.6   Seek Out Help If You Are Struggling Academically

Just about every college and university offers tutoring these days, usually for free. A few years ago, all faculty members at a college where I worked were required to spend three hours a week in the campus tutoring center. We were eager to help, and were hoping we would make a huge difference in the success of our student body. Announcements were made across campus that faculty, not just student tutors, from across the breadth of subjects offered on campus would be in the tutoring center all day long. No appointments were necessary.

There was just one problem – hardly anybody came in. Those who did were mostly the "A" students who really didn't need the help. A handful of students would come in before a test in a "drive-by" attempt to get tutoring. We found it extremely difficult to tutor those students in an hour over a month's worth of material.

Be honest with yourself about whether you need tutoring and, if you do, don't be too proud to seek it out. It's possible that your tutor might be able to explain some concepts better than the professor did. The same goes for campus writing centers. They will undoubtedly help you become a better writer. You may have access also to "virtual" tutoring, whereby you can go online and get tutoring in real time or submit work that will be assessed and sent back to you.

14.7   Make It A Point To Visit Campus Resumé And Job-Interviewing Resources, And Not Just During Your Last Semester Of College

Institutions of higher learning, especially those that receive federal funding, are coming under increasing pressure to place their graduates into jobs. As a result, offices are popping up that evaluate your resumé and provide tips on how to improve and professionalize it. They also offer mock interviewing, after which they provide feedback as to how well or how poorly you conducted yourself. You'll definitely come out a better interviewee and increase your odds of landing a job.

Don't wait until a month before graduation to seek this help. Go throughout your college years so that you can practice these skills when interviewing for on-campus or summer employment. Of all the weaknesses I have personally observed among so-called professionals over the last ten years, this is at the top of the list. I've suffered through countless, downright pathetic interviews by applicants with the most advanced degrees and strongest resumés. It never ceases to amaze me just how many people interview poorly. The job candidate with lesser credentials who interviews well will almost always get hired over the candidate with better credentials whose interview was a train wreck.

All I can think to myself every time a recent graduate stumbles badly through the interview is, "$100,000 of your family's money, four years of your life, and thousands of hours of studying all came down to this, and you've totally blown it." It bears emphasizing – *all of the education in the world is a complete waste if you cannot properly sell yourself in the job market.*

A few years ago I attended an academic-advising seminar at a university in a neighboring state. The dental school faculty from that university conducted a round-table discussion that was supposed to be about advisement in professional schools' academic programs. Instead, it turned into a team tirade about how horribly the dental school applicants conduct themselves in their admissions interviews. Don't overlook the fact that you might have to interview for graduate school, and your interview skills will play a role in whether or not you get accepted.

14.8 If You Are Receiving Financial Aid, Get To Know A Financial Aid Officer And Be Encyclopedic About The Aid You Are Receiving

Many of you are going to college on a "full ride" – a scholarship that covers just about all of your expenses. Some of you may get partial scholarships. Others might receive grants or student loans. Many students fall into several of these categories and have a one-of-a-kind financial aid package.

It is your responsibility to take care of all details related to your aid, regardless of whether you are on full scholarship or just taking out a small loan. Know all of the due dates for paperwork and get it completed in full and on time. Be sure to find out when the funds will be disbursed and what they cover. Every semester I have students who do not have books the first week because they missed a financial aid deadline and have not received the money yet. Be aware of how your aid might change over time, and how many credits you are required to carry and complete.

Nearly all scholarships and grants require you to maintain a minimum GPA. *It is your responsibility to earn it, not your professors' responsibility to give it to you.* Students come to my office near the end of the semester in a panic because they are earning a bad grade and are in danger of losing financial aid. If you are in danger of losing your financial aid because of grades, this problem started way before you met me. You've had plenty of time to bring up your GPA since you started having problems. Never ask a professor for a higher grade for financial aid reasons. I've even had former students come to me several semesters later to ask if I'll change a grade because they are going to lose a scholarship. There is no legal or ethical way I could do that.

Epilogue

Congratulations! Whether you're a high school student or you're coming back to college after a decades-long hiatus, you're now officially ready for college. Many of the issues and advice highlighted in this book may have been complete surprises to you. There was nothing about SAT preparation, selecting a college or filling out an application. "I had no idea I shouldn't do *that* in college," you might have said to yourself many times while you pored over this book. It's far preferable to being blindsided with dozens of unforeseen pitfalls while you're in the throes of your college studies. Now you have a plan of action for tackling problems that might jump in your path. Even better, you have the tools to avoid them.

Everybody gets something different out of the college experience. Students attend college for many different reasons and have a wide variety of goals. The trick is to maximize the opportunities in front of you while minimizing the negatives. Nothing is scarier than the thought of spending tens of thousands of dollars, especially if they're borrowed, only to regret the entire endeavor. Believe me, the college you attend wants your experience to be life changing. After all, they'll be calling you for donations in a few years. *Good luck!*

About The Author

Kent Cubbage is an educator, speaker, and educational consultant who resides in Aiken, S.C. He holds a Ph.D. in educational administration and a graduate certificate in higher education leadership, as well as two degrees in life sciences. He has been a department chair, academic program coordinator, and full-time and adjunct professor at the undergraduate and graduate level. Prior to working in higher education, he spent many years in the corporate world as an environmental consultant. In addition, he is a community leader and professional tour guide.

/128/P

9 781533 583864